Preachers'

Kids

Preachers' Kids

Living in Glass Houses

Rev. Dr. Arnetha Bowens

ABM Media
South Carolina | Pennsylvania | Maryland

Unless otherwise indicated; Scripture quotations used in this book are from The Holy Bible, Authorized King James Version (KJV). Scripture quotations noted AMP are from The Amplified Bible. Similarly, Scripture quotations noted MSG are from The Message Bible.

Library of Congress Cataloging-in-Publication
Data is Available.

ISBN-13: 978-149129260
ISBN-10: 14912926010

Published in the United States of America.

First edition
10   9   8   7   6   5   4   3   2   1

Dedication

Dedicated to the memory of my righteous parents: Bishop George Law Bowens, Jr. and Mother Mary Ruth Bowens with fond memories. Thank you both for rearing my siblings and me as you did. Your children and grandchildren call you both blessed. Again thank you. Your love, care and concern for all of us will always be appreciated and remembered.

This book, also, is dedicated to The Children of The Reverend Clergy. To all Preachers' Kids and Children of Those Who Serve: "Living in Glass Houses;" feeling trapped and don't know how to get out; this book is for you!

৯৯৯৯

Bishop George Law Bowens, Jr. & Mother Mary Ruth Bowens

Acknowledgments

A Time to Say: Thanks . . .

Special thanks to my dynamic siblings: Bishop/Pastor Joseph P. Bowens; Missionary Helen Gray; Minister James R. Bowens, Sr.; Bernice Oakman, BSN and Martie Martin, Education Advocate. I have been truly blessed by your love, prayers and support. Your words of encouragement are highly valued. I have learned so much from all of you. Much love to the blessed memory of my sister, Missionary Margaret Hardeman and my brother, Evangelist David Bowens, Sr. You are the very best family anyone could ever have. I love and appreciate each and every one of you, for being you. Thanks for loving me, for me, with all of my idiosyncrasies.

Affectionate enjoyment and appreciation to my fervent prayer support team: Abigail Hurley and Dominic Hurley, II. *"But Jesus said, Suffer little children, and forbid them not, to come unto me: for of such is the kingdom of heaven."* (Matthew 19:14)

Loving gratitude to my faithful 'Prayer Partners': Minister Lynne Galloway, Missionary Helen Gray, Pastor Linda Grissett, Minister Vera Hawley, Evangelist Elizabeth Hutchings, Missionary Dollie Diane Taylor and Dr. Joseph L. Ross, Sr. You are a God-sent blessing and inspiration to me. Thanks for being in prayer for and with me, while I worked on this book.

Special thanks to my nieces and nephews: Jeanette Hardeman, Joy Hurley, David L. Bowens, Jr., Gerald A. Martin, Jr. and Gerome Martin.

Sincere appreciation to Mr. Charles Lanier and Ms. Marsha Stroman, for their significant contributions in helping me get this book published.

Thanks to everyone who shared precious ingredients of their life stories. They reminisced and mused over the good, the awful, the unattractive and the better, while growing up as Preachers' Kids; also known as, Children of The Reverend Clergy. Evangelist Maudesta Claiborne, Ms. Sylvia Davis, Missionary Helen Gray, Missionary Joy Hurley, Ms. Sylvia Long, Ms. Carolyn Mole, Mrs. Tracey Pryce and The Reverend Janice Roberts; thank you. Your heartwarming testimonies will help encourage others who are members of this select alliance – PKs. Words cannot express my heartfelt gratitude to all of you.

Finally, thank you, Martie, for believing in me and helping me put this baby to bed (print language for getting this book published). Again, thank you.

A Prayer of Thanks

Father God, You are awesome! You heard and answered my prayer. Thank You, Lord, for all You have done, are doing and will do for me. I love, honor and adore You. Use this book for Your glory to make a difference across America, and around the world in the lives of men, women, boys and girls. Amen. Amein.

Table of Contents

Table of Contents (continued)

Table of Contents (continued)

Table of Contents (continued)

Note: Initial Caps are intentionally used for such words as: Bishop, Children, Church, Citizen, Dad, Mom, Glass House, Ministry, Offspring, Parent(s) Pastor, Preachers' Kids, Priest, Public Servants, Royalty, Synagogue, The Reverend Clergy and the like; aimed at an emphatic effect.

Preachers' Kids

Living In Glass Houses

Preface

This book is written to the Children of The Reverend Clergy, as well as, Public Servants, who have likewise, dedicated their lives to the service of humanity. This exemplary group daily serves among us; professionally doing their jobs, as Public Servants. These amazing Citizens are willing to respond to human need, at any moment, at any happening, at times, putting their own lives at risk.

In spite of everything, many who serve, may come from humble beginnings and have very little wealth. Nonetheless, they give their lives to the call of God; to Minister and care for the need of others. These extraordinary people come from all religions, faiths and denominations. As one, they are collectively recognized, as The Reverend Clergy. This is the purpose for which this book was written. Together, all of these Children are tucked-in under an ageless, giant alliance umbrella, termed "Preachers' Kids". We are indebted to all of them; all of us, both religious and secular. Pain hurts, no matter the cause, or the situation. Hence, we offer all of you; all of us, an eternal: "*We Love You*".

Over and over again, Children of The Reverend Clergy, as well as family members, are repeatedly, referred to as:

- Bench warmer
- Church-goer
- Fault finder
- Goody-goody
- Goody two-shoes
- Grundy

- Holier-than-thou
- Holy Joe
- Nice Nelly
- Self-righteous
- Rabbis' Kids
- PKs
- Politicos' Kids
- Preachers' Kids
- Puritan
- Wowser.

On occasion, the name calling and taunting seem endless. Countless cruel acts, and unkind hurtful words are hurled toward innocent Children, simply due to the occupations of their Parents, and/or family members. Accordingly, Children of Athletes and Entertainers may experience the same kind of spitefulness and intimidations.

Perhaps, you were born into a religious family? Maybe, you were adopted by a political family? Perchance, you were given to a family in professional sport, as a foster child? No matter the situation; it was by no fault of your own. You played no part in the decision-making. Although we have no choice in its' membership; it does not matter. The PK alliance is perpetual; consisting of all peoples, cultures and customs. It is ageless, color-blind and global.

This book is for you. This book is for me. It is written to you. It is written to me. It attempts to address issues, problems and situations that challenge all of us. I know you have questions about your family member's call to help others; while your family may need a little consideration. Some of your conflicts, (our conflicts) may have resided in and with you, (us) since childhood. These uncertainties may include unresolved struggles ranging from: who we are, to what is the purpose of our life. You may wonder how I know? Very simply, I am, like many of you – a Preachers' Kid.

Enjoy

Rev. Dr. Arnetha Bowens

WELCOME

This Book belongs to:

_____

Date: _____

Gift given by:_____

Date: _____

Comments: _____

_____

_____

*"The blessing of the LORD, it maketh rich, and He addeth
no sorrow with it."* (Proverbs 10:22)

"O TASTE AND SEE THAT THE LORD

IS GOOD: BLESSED IS THE MAN

THAT TRUSTETH IN HIM."

Psalm 34:8

Preachers' Kids

Our Only Wish Is To Be Normal

Chapter 1

We are Children of The Reverend Clergy. A member of our family may be a Cleric, a Nun, a Deacon, an Elder, a Mother of the Church, or perhaps a Choir member. You see, our alliance is all-embracing extensive, inclusive, distinctive and influential. There are no external features, nor internal attributes that can separate us. We come in all ages, sizes, ethnicities, professions, class and cultures. We are all together. We are one. We all share the same 'PK' pigeonhole. It doesn't matter the color of our eyes; how much we look like Uncle; the hue of our skin; where we live; how high we can jump; nor the amount of sinful acts we participate in, or involve ourselves; we are all marked – PK! Our only brand is and always will be: "Preachers' Kids". All of us, collectively have been and always will be seared with an ageless hot iron, PKs: "One of them." "So you think you're so much – the *'Holy Ones'*. We'll show you!"

Remember the story of Peter's denial of his dear friend, Jesus. Until then, he appeared to be a loyal and faithful Disciple of Jesus. Yet, in the end, he could not break away from his prior allegiance to Jesus and his fellow Apostles. No matter how Peter, (often looked up to as a 'Rock'), tried to obscure himself, he could not escape the scrutiny of being discovered: "One of Them!!"

Luke 22:54b-60a writes about a man in conflict with his own faith. When faced with his acclaimed religious conviction, this close friend of Jesus, 'wish at heart', was to fade away into the crowd. It reads: *"And Peter followed afar off. And when they had kindled a fire in the midst of the hall, and were set down together, Peter sat down among them. But a certain maid beheld him as he sat by the fire, and earnestly looked upon him, and said, This man was also with Him. And he denied Him, saying, Woman, I know Him not. And after a little while another saw him, and said, Thou art also of them. And Peter said, Man, I am not. And about the space of one hour after another confidently affirmed, saying, Of a truth this fellow also was with Him: for he is a Galilean. And Peter said, Man, I know not what thou sayest.."*

As Preachers' Kids, how often, do we follow our Parents, and/or family members from afar? Sometimes, people may recognize us, and ask: "Don't I know you"? Frequently, the reply is, "I don't think so". Not convinced, they may say, "Yes, you are the Pastor's child". We may respond, "I don't know what you are talking about. Everyone has a twin." Returning home, we are met head-on with, "why did you mislead that dear Lady"? There is always a 'duty hotline' to PKs' families. Before arriving back home, our Parents would receive telephone calls, as to our behavior. "Our intent was not to deceive her. We simply didn't validate her guess.

The PK brand belongs to the Children of those who work to make the quality of life better and easier for others. Our Parents, and family members are those who serve in every area of life, sharing of themselves and making improvements wherever they can. It does not matter what their titles are, we have one thing in common. We are the Children of those who contribute their lives to service. Our Parents and families are those on the front line, always on display, always on call. Year-in, year-out, month-in, month-out, day-by-day, throughout all seasons, life cycles, ceremonies, sacraments, life struggles, sorrows, joys and celebrations; The Reverend Clergy usually serve for their entire lives. Their vocations spread far and wide across all nations, cultures, nationalities, traditions, religious affiliations and into all the world. These Holy men and women serve as Pastors, Bishops, Elders, Evangelists, Nuns, Teachers, Rabbis, Cantors, Rectors, Chaplains, Missionaries, Ministers, Prophets, Priests and Inspirational Leaders. Their Cleric duties consist of, but are not limited to:

- Always Praying
- Baptisms
- Births

- Blessings
- Charity
- Christenings
- Counseling
- Daycare
- Education
- Fasting
- Feeding the Hungry
- Fundraising
- Funerals
- Holiday Celebrations
- Holy Days' Observances
- Hospitality
- Preaching
- Sacraments
- Sermonize
- Visiting the Prisons
- Visiting the Sick
- Weddings; etc., etc.
- Praying Continually.

As a result, here we are the family and Children of The Reverend Clergy. Frequently, we never get to really know them. Nonetheless, as their Children, we were born to live in '*Glass Houses*' with them. Our directives are to live righteous, supportive, exemplary lives; always cognizant that we are PKs. A family member of The Reverend Clergy told me, that their three Children only had two public requirements.

The first essential is a reflection from Proverbs 22:1. "*A good <u>name</u> is rather to be chosen than great riches, and loving favor rather than silver and gold.*" The Children were told: "Keep our name clean". The second essential is a prayer from Psalm 25:2. "*O my God, I trust in thee: let me not be <u>ashamed,</u> let not mine enemies triumph over me.*" The Children were told that they could party hardy like they just didn't care; but while they were at it, they were advised: "Don't make us ashamed." Today, they are all adults. Yet, these essential specifics are forever branded onto their souls and in their conscience.

"LET THE WORDS OF MY MOUTH, AND THE MEDICATION OF MY HEART, BE ACCEPTABLE IN THY SIGHT, O LORD, MY STRENGTH, AND MY REDEEMER."

Psalm 19:14

Accept Me For Me!!! Let Me Be Me!!!

Chapter 2

We are Children of The Reverend Clergy. Please, allow me to let
you in on a little secret. Our lives and the lives of our families are
continuously scrutinized. We hurt. We loose hope. We wish for, and
want love and acceptance. We want to be celebrated; not tolerated.
As quiet as it is kept, at times, we look for love in all the wrong
places. The same desire may be true for many of you. When we get
discouraged, it eats at the very core of our being. We sometimes
become like the prodigal son who squandered his inheritance on
riotous living. After sowing our wild oats, we often get angry with
ourselves. We blame God. We blame our Parents. We blame other
people. We blame John Q Public. We even blame the Church, rather
than taking responsibility for our own mistakes. The Children of
'Those Who Serve' want acceptance for who we are, and *NOT* for
who, and what our Parents are. We have flesh on our bones, and
blood running warm in our veins; the same as all of you. Our basic
human needs are the same as the next person: food, clothing and
shelter. Nonetheless, most of all, we desire love and respect.

People tend not to let us be on our own. They want us to
become replicas of our Parent(s), grandparents and/or guardians.
We are likely to be 'off-ended' by their 'fishing' platitudes all the
time. For example, why are you not like your parents? Why are you
not helping more in Ministry with your Parents? Are you really
saved? Do you know Jesus? Your Parents need you to help them in
the Ministry. People want to believe that Children of The Reverend
Clergy were born into Ministry to Minister. This experience is
comparable for most of the Children in the PK alliance.

5

Our spirits cry out, we are individuals, not Preachers, nor Deacons nor Choir members. We are Children of The Reverend Clergy. Our sobs and whimpers (often silent) is ACCEPT ME FOR ME!!! Accept Us! Let ME Be ME!!! Please allow me to pursue my personal dreams and aspiration, not yours, nor theirs. Are you willing to permit me to reach for my desired vision? I have something to offer humanity. I have special gifts, talents and abilities. Let me off your predetermined merry-go-round, to search for my explicit life work. LISTEN to me!!! I have something to say. STOP comparing me to my Parents, and/or my grandparents. Stop comparing me to my brothers, sisters, and/or cousins! STOP comparing me with other peoples' Kids. Most of all STOP comparing me with your Kids.

STOP! LOOK! LISTEN! LOOK AT ME NOW. I AM an individual. As quiet as it is kept, God has given me brilliance, personality and amazing skills. I am grateful that God bequested wisdom, knowledge and understanding into my life. Listen to what I have to say. I want to be heard. I am not a clone of my Parents, or my grandparents. I am an individual. I love life and want to find my way. I desire to fulfill the intentions of my heart. Please, do not hinder me from reaching my destiny. God is ordering my steps. Stop throwing hindrances of any kind in my path. I am tired of 'Living in a Glass House'. Give me some privacy. Allow me to interact with other people, without constant analysis, criticism, or review. If you refuse to help me; then do not hinder or obstruct my progress.

Lives Ending In Tragedy

I heard this story a few years ago. The son of a Pastor went to Vietnam, fought in the war and returned home a drug addict. He never recuperated from the affects of war. In the year of 2000, he went to his Parents' home and shot himself to death in the family room. This young man committed suicide. He found himself unable to handle the residual pressure from the war, and what was expected of him when he returned. Everyone expected him to be strong like his Dad, the Pastor. He may have had personal trepidations that were not dealt with. He was desperately in need of help and emotional healing.

The people around him, who loved him most, namely his family, may not have been aware, how close he was, to giving up. The help he possibly needed, may not have reached him in a timely fashion. Bottom line: He saw suicide as his only option, to ease the pain. He checked out of this world. The pressures tended to be too much for him to manage. How painful for this son, and the family he left behind. Can you image finding the body of a loved one, who has committed suicide? Let's pray that, by the Grace of God, we never will. I am sure it was a difficult pill to swallow for this precious family. The tragedy must have been devastating, not only for a family of The Reverend Clergy, but for any family experiencing such a lost.

Another Story

The Reverend Oral Roberts and his wife, Evelyn, 'bless their memory', were on Pastor Benny Hinn's program, many years ago. He and his wife gave a testimony about one of their sons taking his life. He couldn't handle the memory of Vietnam and the way the Soldiers were treated upon their return to the United States. People are hurting today, especially those 'Living in Glass Houses'. The pain can be excruciating and many times unbearable.

Some of the Children of the Clerics who serve, sometimes walk away from their families, the LORD, the Church and anything analogous to religion. Many may have left family businesses and traditional lifestyles. They felt that the pressures of life akin to religion were too much to endure. Some of the people, you see sleeping on the streets are not homeless. Many, just put a few things in a shopping bag, walked out the door and said good-bye to life, as they knew it. They would rather drop out from the social order of community. They leave behind the Church, the LORD and the family business – Ministry. I can hear the wheels turning in your heads, asking why? Why would someone do such a thing? Why would they walk away from family, friends, Church, Synagogue, and/or God? Leaving your support group is unheard of. Why walk away from all you have into a life that is unknown?

Who can influence you to do such a thing? Let me tell you who. It is the enemy of your soul, the devil. He is influencing you to do such distressful things to yourself. That is why people tend to hurt those they love and those who love them. Who is your enemy? Your enemy is the devil, and his co-horts. Many people are miserable and unhappy. They want others to be miserable as well. John 10:10 illustrates, three devices the devil makes use of in dealing with humanity. Jesus said, "The thief cometh not, but for to steal, and to kill, and to destroy: I am come that they might have life, and that they might have it more abundantly". I am so glad that Jesus came, that we might have an overflowing life and have it more abundantly. Hallelujah.

Chapter 3

How do you see yourself? What is the image you see in the mirror? Will you be made whole? Do you have the mental accruement to be made whole? Do you see yourself whole? Complete? Jesus asked the impotent man who sat by the pool having an infirmity for 38 years this question. Wilt thou be made whole? Immediately, the man started giving Him excuses why he was still in that state. He sat beside that pool with an infirmity for 38 years, more than three decades. Someone must have fed him. Someone had to wash him and his clothing. It stands to reason that someone was taking care of his basic human needs. When you examine his situation, looks like he had a hustle going on. He gave Jesus an excuse when asked the question, *"Will thou be made whole"?*

Are you making excuses for not moving forward? What excuses are you using for sitting on the stool of do nothing, whistling to the tune of do less? What excuses are you giving yourself for not going forward with God, and the things of God? What excuses are you using for leaving the family business? Do you have a hustle going on? Do some self-inventory. First, "to thine own self be true".

Let's Talk

Our Cleric Parents were chosen, and called by God, to Preach, the *Good News* of the Gospel of Jesus Christ to a lost and dying world. We did not think they were always there for us, but they were. It appeared as if the people at Church and in the community had and

9

still have our Parents more than us. The question on the floor is: Why do you think that is true? I can hear your responses. Someone was always in our home and/or on our telephone, taking our Parents' time away from us. When our family would have an outing, people would come up to our Parents and monopolize their time. This would take their minds off of the event and our family. We came to resent the Ministry, the business, their career and the people ruining our family outings. Do you think this was communicated to our Parents? Most times, it was not. Telling our parents was not an option. We did not want our Parents to feel badly. After all, they were doing the LORD's work, or working to take care of the family. Does that sound right?

Some of us did not discuss our displeasure with our siblings either. These feelings were oft times suppressed. Our feeling that God would be displeased with us was ever present. There was a fear that God would zap us if we voiced our displeasure with our parents. Some of us questioned why God chose our parent(s) to work in His Ministry? Why didn't He choose our neighbors or anyone else but our parents? Why were our Parents always in the limelight? Why weren't they just white or blue-collar workers? They didn't have to own the place. The enemy of our souls is constantly talking in our ears, trying to put negative thoughts in our minds. That negativity is rehearsed over and over again. As we rehearse it, negativity gets down into our hearts and spirits. The evil one is constantly throwing accusations in our minds toward our Parents, not loving and being there for us.

Proverbs 6:31: *"But if he be found, he shall restore sevenfold; he shall give all the substance of his house."*

He tries to convince you that your situation would have been different if your Parents were there. If only they were not Preachers, you would be loved more. They would have more time for you. You could have done this, that or the other, together. People try to convince us that we are not important to our Parents. Others are more important. If Dad and Mom really cared about us, they would stay home with us. They would not accept all of the interviews, Radio time, films, and/or engagements. They would tell the 'do-drop-inners' to go home. This is not a good time to visit. You must leave now. The next time, please call before you come.

Was this your life? Is this your life now? Did your Parents continuously leave you with a sitter? Are you constantly on the road with them not getting enough rest? Is your answer a resounding YESSSSSSSSSSSSSSSS? A thousand times YES. That is and was my life. But, you see, we thought it would have been sacrilegious if they didn't allow people to intrude upon their rights and privacy. Is that your thought processes? Is it a requirement from God to always be available for the masses? It is the right thing to do, right? The talents your Parents have came from God. Didn't they? They are using these talents to provide for us and to help others. Right?

We question why they are allowing this intrusion of our privacy? Why can't we live a normal life like everyone else? Dad was brilliant and very charismatic. He could have chosen another profession. Why didn't he become a doctor, lawyer, teacher or Indian chief? He didn't have to become a Preacher, a Rabbi, an actor or a politician. Mom was also brilliant. Why didn't she pursue greatness in other areas of her life? Why did she feel the need to Preach, instead of act, sing, teach and/or go into commerce? Just because my family is from the Tribe of Levi, did that mean my Parents had to become members of the Rabbinical Priesthood? Does that mean I am called to carry out those same duties? I love God and the things of God but I prefer to be in the background, not out front. I am always on display. What's up with that? Children of 'those who serve' enjoy very little private time with their Parents. Regularly, others infringe upon our family times. God gave us our Parents. He wants us to be happy. I know God loves us. The questions on the floor are: "How much longer? When will this all end? Can I please have some 'me' time?" These are a few unspoken questions, you maybe too fearful of God to voice out loud.

Let me explain something to you. God is Omnipotent – all-powerful, possessing complete, unlimited. He is universal in power and authority. God is Omniscient, all-knowing. He is Omnipresent – continuously and simultaneously present throughout the whole of the whole of creation, everywhere present at the same time. God sees all, hears all, knows all and is in all. There is nothing hidden from Him. We would be petrified if we focus on these facts about God. It is all about us. We are so focused on the things that we feel we should have but do not. The facts about the character of God never enter our minds. It is all about us. Know this: God loves you so much that He sent Jesus to die that you might live the abundant life.

Another thing: Stop comparing yourself with Joe Smo, Suzie Q and Lucie Lou. It is wrong for us to compare ourselves with others. The Bible tells us plainly:

"For we dare not make ourselves of the number, or compare ourselves with some that commend themselves: but they measuring themselves by themselves, and comparing themselves among themselves, are not wise."

(II Corinthians 10:12)

Are you comparing your family with others? Do you think their family structure is better than yours? They appear to be so happy. Right? Reality check. The 80/20 rule. Leaving/longing for the 20, when you have the 80 in hand. Why leave the 80 for the 20? The grass always looks greener on the other side until you get there. You will find that the grass is dead. The perfect family unit on the outside has some dysfunction inside. Your home environment may not be perfect according to you, but neither is theirs. Everyone has some growing to do. In every home, there is disagreement if people live in them. No home is perfect, although we strive for perfection. Enough is enough. Oh, God, please get me out of this *'Glass House'* is your constant plea.

12

Preachers' Kids

The Worst Kind of What?

Chapter 4

Hey, let's have some dialogue? It is time to talk. We need an understanding. Are you there? Children of The Reverend Clergy have the same needs and desires as other Children. *Right?* We desire to be loved and cared for by others. Do you follow? We are Children, born as you were born, who also desire the finer things of life. Still the same with us! We have goals, dreams, and visions. Let us be. Set us free to be men and women, boys and girls. Set us free. Let us enjoy life. Stop trying to take our wings away from us. When you see us attempting to fly, will you help us? Stop with the constant put down and discouragement. Your derogatory words and frowns cut us deep. It sometimes cut to the very core of our being. How many of you have been accused of being *'the worst kind'*?

The statement: *"Preachers' Kids Are The Worst Kind"*. can hurt you to your heart. It causes one to query this. *"We are the worst kind of what?"* What made us *the worst*? Why would God make us *'the worst kind'*? Out of all of the people in the world, we were picked to be *'the worst kind'* in the entire world. Why? This question is plaguing Children of The Reverend Clergy until this day. *"We are the worst kind of what?"* Why would such a harmful, negative label be put on Children due to the vocation of their Parents? We would like this statement explained to us.

That statement was first made to me, by a high school teacher. I raised my hand to be excused. Permission was refused. I knew the consequences if I didn't leave the room. My response was: "All due respect, I must be excused." As I left the room the response was *"I always knew that Preachers' Kids are the worst kind"*.

13

Those words rang in my ears as I left the class. Some of the students laughed at the statement. I felt bad. My mind went over that statement. I pondered *"the worst kind of what"*? What were they talking about, *"the worst kind"*? I only asked to be excused in a respectful manner. *"The worst kind of what?"* I will never forget that class.

As my day progressed, I changed classes. During an afternoon class, I asked to be excused for the same reason. Again, my request was denied. My response was the same. "All due respect I must be excused." As I arose from my desk to leave the room, I heard the same words I had heard earlier echoing in my ears: *"I always knew that Preachers' Kids are the worst kind"? Worst kind of what?* What are we doing as 'Preachers' Kids' that make us so bad? What and/or who are we being compared? In the ladies room while washing my hands, I thought about this statement. Twice in one day, I am being ridiculed by an authority figure, someone I am supposed to look up to in life. What do they see in me? What do they see in us that would cause them to make such a statement? Are we involved in something outrageous? Why are we ostracized in our own communities, cities, states and the world? I looked at myself in the mirror trying to see what they saw. I wanted to know what they saw in me, and others like me, that made us *"the worst kind"*. I thought I was a Southern Belle. I was an honor roll student. I didn't smoke, drink, gamble, whore around, kill, steal, or lie. I tried to be a model Citizen. I was not immoral. I spoke my mind. I said what I thought pretty much. Did that make me *"the worst kind"*?

When I went home from school that day, my Mom was there, waiting for her Children, with a delicious homemade before dinner snack. I told her about my traumatic experiences in two of my classes. Mom listened very attentively to me. She assured me this matter would be dealt with immediately. My Dad arrived home from work and dinner was served shortly, thereafter. Later in the evening, we had our usual family time. Dad, Mom and some of the Kids sat in chairs while others sat on the floor.

Dad re-iterated to us, that we should never let anyone put us down because of who we are, what we do, or what we do not have, nor because of the color of our skin, size or whatever. We are as good as, and/or better than anyone walking on two feet. In fact, "We are Preachers' Kids". Dad asked about our day. I told Dad what happened at school. My Dad, a very wise man, a loving protective husband, and father asked me how I felt about what was said to me. I explained to my Dad the impact that statement had on me. After analyzing the statement, my question to Dad was, *"We are the worst kind of what"*? I do not understand why this is said to us and about us. During our early years, my siblings had similar experiences. "O how I miss my Dad and Mom." They have both transitioned into their new home in Heaven. May God bless their memory.

Dad's explanation helped us to see things from a different perspective. Picture this: It was the segregated South. Professionals in the then Negro (African American) community did not receive the same respect as The Reverend Clergy received from other races, including their own race. The Reverend Clergy received much more respect than the teachers, doctors, lawyers and other professionals in the African American community. As a result of The Reverend Clergy in our community receiving more respect than many who had graduated college; resentment was perceived among the ranks. The Reverend Clergy in our community, and their Offspring were now and then, looked upon with disdain, until there was a need for their services. Maybe, just maybe, this is the source of that erroneous statement: *"Preachers' Kids Are The Worst Kind"*. Again the question on the floor is: *"Worst kind of what"?*

The next day, my Mom went to the school and spoke with the principal as well as all of my teachers, especially the two who made the derogatory statement the day before. After Mom's visit, I never heard that statement from any other authority figure. Dad and Mom assured me the day it happened that the situation would be dealt with immediately and it was. My Dad encouraged his Children to be direct and tell the truth. I tried to obey him with everything that was in me. I was straight to the point. We could not talk back or sass anyone. Hence, sassing our Elders was not and is not an option. It was seen as disrespect. Yet, we are considered the worst kind. *The worst kind of what?* All of us didn't curse, swear and act a fool. We did not steal nor kill. But we are on display as being *'the worst kind'* *"We are Living in a Glass House."* No matter what we do, or what we say, at times we are ridiculed.

There were Children in our town who were having abortions, whoring around, drinking like a fish, committing adultery with married men and women, stealing, spending time in jail, smoking, drinking and carousing. Yet, we, the Preachers' Kids are considered *'the worst kind'*. *"The worst kind of what?"* It is repeatedly said, we, the Preachers' Kids are *'the worst kind'*. *"The worst kind of what?"* We are always on display. People are expecting the worst of us. When they are questioned regarding our behavior, the response is didn't you know that *"Preachers' Kids Are The Worst Kind"*? What is the criterion that they are using? We are under close scrutiny at all times. No matter what we do and or say, we are criticized. If we bought into that negativity, one would believe that they cannot do anything right. But we know that is not true. We are God-fearing, loving, smart, honest individuals who happen to live in *'Glass Houses'*. Know in your knower that you are fearfully and wonderfully made in the image and likeness of God, Our Heavenly Father.

When we take our rightful place becoming an integral part of the Ministry with our Parents, we are often ostracized and ridiculed. Many have been heard saying: Who do they think they are? Every time I turn around, they are up doing this, that and the other. They are working on my nerves, always on display. They are parading in and out of the Church, on and off the scene. They are taking up the offerings, ushering, and singing on the choir, entertaining us. I am tired of them. They sit their children at the organ and piano and let them bang. They are not that talented. They can play. Why them and not my Children? They think their Children are better than anyone else. Every chance I get I let them know, that they are not all that. My little Jimmie is not given a chance and I am not going to take it anymore. Enough is enough*!!*

16

When we, the Children of 'Those Who Serve', do not participate in the Church and its activities, we are called '*the worst kind*'. When we sit quietly in the pews, we are called '*the worst kind*'. When we are mischievous, we are '*the worst kind*'. When we participate in all of the Church activities, we are '*the worst kind*'. No matter what we do, it is not good enough. Will you help me? Help us? We need clarity. We, Preachers' Kids, need an understanding. Why do you all hate us so much? Why do you all dislike us so much? Why are accusatory fingers being pointed in our direction? We will never do anything to hurt you deliberately. We are hurting because of the way you treat us. What is the problem? We, the Preachers' Kids are considered '*the worst kind*'. My question still is: *"We are the worst kind of what?"*

What will it take for you to accept us as human beings? We bleed the same red blood; breathe the same air. Let us blossom into the men and women, boys and girls God wants us to be. God has a plan and purpose for us; we desire to live in accordant. Will you help us? Your little Johnnie gets into trouble. You say they are *worst* than you. They do things *worst* than this. Again, what are you referring to? Where did this statement *"Preachers' Kids are the worst kind"* originate? *We are the worst kind?* What's the source?

I asked that question of one of my friends. This is the answer I received. "So much is expected from you all as Preachers' Kids because of who your Parents are. The fact, you were raised by The Reverend Clergy, suggests that you should have more than average morals and values. High standards must always be demonstrated in every facet of our lives. Moral expectations are high. Given this is not the case, our Parents should be held more accountable. They ought to keep a better watchful eye on us. Reverend Clergy Parents should be more loving and accessible to their children. Nevertheless, they must remain welcoming and reachable to their Parishioners. Again, the question on the floor is *"We are the worst kind of what"*?

PKs , just because we are labeled as '*the worst kind*', it doesn't make it so nor true. Say what God says about you.

"AS FAR AS THE EAST IS FROM

THE WEST, SO FAR HATH

HE REMOVED OUR

TRANSGRESSIONS FROM US."

Psalm 99:12

Forgive The Offenders

Chapter 5

Pssst. Pssst. Pssst. I am calling the Children of: "Those Who Serve" in: Ministry, politics, entertainment, sport as well as any spotlight worker. I refer to these Children and family members as *"Those Who Live in Glass Houses"*. Bishops, Pastors, Rabbis, Priests together with all Clerics. This call is for you. I know you have been hurt by the masses. This hurt has been going on for quite some time. It has reached the core of your being. Forgive the antagonist. Forgive those who have hurt you. Forgive those who are hurting you now. Get over it. Forgive the Church members who have made digs at you and your family for generations. Forgive all of the negativity that is aimed at you. The time is now to forgive those who have hurt you. They have gone on with their lives and you are still holding on to their garbage. It is eating you alive from the inside out. Take your life back. One of my aunts always said: *"Give me back my business so I can go on my way"*. Take your life back.

Jesus told us that if we do not forgive, neither will our Heavenly Father forgive us our trespasses. Forgive. Ask God to forgive those individuals who hurt you and help the hurts to stop hurting. We must forgive. Many would trade places with you today if they could. Remember, people only make digs at someone they want to be like. Someone wants to emulate you. See the big picture. People will come at you from all angles, but do not let them discourage you. God is on your side. You can make it.

19

In Luke 11:1b, *"One of His disciples said unto Him, LORD, teach us to pray, as John also taught his disciples"*. Jesus instructed them how to pray. Verse 4 says, *"And forgive us our sins; for we also forgive every one that is indebted to us. And lead us not into temptation; but deliver us from evil"*.

Example:

I was told a story about two men in an office. One was a young man who was about to graduate from college. The other was an elderly man. He was encouraging the graduate to do all and be all he could do and be. He took the younger man to the window. As they looked out, the elderly gentleman asked this question, *"What do you see?"* The response was: *"I see two trees"*. *Look a little closer at the trees. "I see a pecan tree and a chinaberry tree." "Is there anything different about the tree, other than the fruit?" "Yes. In the pecan tree, there are all kinds of debris, but in the chinaberry tree, there is nothing but chinaberries."* The young man asked why? The elderly man responded this way. *"People only throw at what they are interested in, something they want."*

So, when people come at you "Children of Those Who Serve": from every angle, *"Rejoice, and be exceeding glad: for great is your reward in heaven: for so persecuted they the prophets which were before you"*. (Matthew 5:12) Do not hold onto insults or offenses. Holding onto wrongdoings can stop or hinder the flow of God's blessings from moving in your lives.

Offence is a condemnation attack weapon that satan trys to use against the Children of God. Stop becoming off-ended with people. Do not allow their issues with life to become your problems. Getting caught up in others lifestyles can hinder your growth and development. Trust in the LORD with all of your heart. When people are throwing everything at you including the kitchen sink, trust God. He will see you through. Shake off the unforgiveness. See God in the midst of it all. See His hand guiding and directing you and yours. God will bring you through your challenges victoriously. Declare: "LORD, I forgive. Help Thou my unforgiveness. LORD, I forgive John. LORD, I forgive Jane Doe. LORD, I forgive".

20

Jesus said: *"For if ye forgive men their trespasses, your heavenly Father will also forgive you: But if ye forgive not men their trespasses, neither will your Father forgive your trespasses."*
(Matthew 6:14-15)

"For I know the thoughts that I think toward you, saith the LORD, thoughts of peace, and not of evil, to bring you an expected end."
(Jeremiah 29:11)

God has good thoughts toward you. He wants great things to happen in your life, but you are allowing unforgiveness to stop it from coming to past in your life. Sure, you may have been hurt by people in your community. You may even have been hurt by Church people, including your family. That is life. Hurt is a reality, not an option. Hurting people, hurt people When we are hurting, we go into a defensive mode. We sometimes go underground into a shelter or a cocoon. We simply shut down. We vow never to let any one get close enough to hurt us ever again. We put our guard up trying to protect ourselves.

Every time someone enters this forbidden territory that you have closed off – they encounter an attitude second to none. You start acting ugly toward them. It is a sad situation. When you think about the person(s) who hurt you, your blood runs cold. Another vow is made. Never again will anyone hurt me. If anything, I will do the hurting from now on. You are trying to protect yourself against being hurt. Impossible! The more you try to hide your feelings, the more vulnerable you are. Unforgiveness will cause you to become angry, defensive, fearful and paranoid. Job 3:25 said, "For t*he thing which I greatly feared is come upon me, and that which I was afraid of is come unto me"* You become like a magnet drawing all of the things you do not desire to yourself. Unforgiveness leads to worst things. All of those things are hindrances to the blessings of the LORD in your lives.

What do you fear? Why are you so angry at Susie Q and/or Joe Blow? When you see Susie Q and/or Joe Blow your blood runs cold. Why? Think about it. They are not affected by your presence

21

at all, but you are affected by theirs. You are holding a grudge. They have gone on with their lives. If you mentioned to them what you are angry at they would look at you as if you were crazy. You are enslaved by your own unforgiveness. It has you in bondage. Forgive everyone who has hurt you, whether they are alive or dead. Put a chair in front of you. Call the person's name. Say Joe Blow, and/or Susie Q, I forgive you. LORD, I forgive them. Help Thou my unforgiveness. Deliver me from any and everything that will not bring glory and honor to You, LORD.

I choose to forgive and forget. I choose total deliverance in every facet of my life. Unforgiveness binds, grips, and dominates a person's life. When a person dwells on the negative, look closely and you will see the error. How can you not forgive someone based upon their offense when Jesus has forgiven you for so much? Do not let any one destroy you. Go to God in prayer and things will change drastically for you.

When the Son makes you free, you shall be free indeed. Does God want you free? Yes, He does. Only God can heal your insides to set you free. Cry out to God today to make you free from the yoke of bondage. Free from torment. Free from anger. Free from everything that has you in bondage. Stand flat-footed on the Word of God. He is the Great Liberator. Depend on Him to make you free.

"And ye shall know the truth, and the truth shall make you free."
(John 8:32)

"If the Son therefore shall make you free, ye shall be free indeed."
(John 8:36)

Let the LORD set you free from the hurts and pains of your past. *"Casting all of your care upon Him; for He careth for you."* (I Peter 5:7) Why are you holding onto the weights of your past? Why have you given that person or those persons so much power over you? You are angry with God, your parents, your selves, situations and so much more. Stop pointing the finger at them and start pointing it at yourselves. You have relinquished your power into the hands of other people. It is time for you to put an end to the blame game. Stop right now. It is eating you alive. Where are you in the scheme of things? What is your part in all of this?

Jesus told us plainly if we do not forgive neither will God forgive us. Unforgiveness will cripple you in every area of your life. Harboring unforgiveness in your heart house is not of God. Realize this is a spiritual battle. The enemy of your soul will build a nest in your mind of unforgiveness. As you meditate on it, the unforgiveness seeps into your heart and goes deep down into your spirit. That thing that has offended you is now controlling you on every hand. What must you do to forgive? Did you say forgive? Yes. Forgive so that God will forgive your trespasses. When Jesus was asked by Peter this question, "How many times should I forgive – seven times? Jesus replied in this manner. No, you should not forgive just seven times, but seventy times seven and all in the same day. The bottom line is to forgive.

Forgive!!! Forgive!!! Forgive!!! Oh! One more thing, forgive! Forgive the offender. Forgive the offense. They do not remember what they did or said. If they do remember what they did to you was wrong and do not apologize for the wrong, so what? Get over it. Do not allow another's issues to become your issues. Why are you holding onto it? It is eating you up like a cancer. It is crippling you. The offender has gone on with their lives. You might say I will forgive but I will not forget. When you rehearse the wrong done to you over and over again, you are giving place to the devil. Jesus told us in the Gospels: If we do not forgive men their trespasses, neither will our Father in heaven forgive us. Forgive. You will feel so much better when you do.

The Bible also encourages us that we should pray without ceasing. Pray for those who have hurt you. Pray for those who have rule over you. Pray for your family and friends. Pray for your country. Pray for the world. Get a prayer partner to agree with you and stand on the promises of God for your situation. Getting some-one to agree with you is one of the hardest things to do. If you can find an Agree-er, apply this scripture when the two of you agree.

"Jesus said, Take this most seriously: A yes on earth is yes in heaven; a no on earth is no in heaven. What you say to one another is eternal. I mean this. When two of you get together on anything at all on earth and make a prayer of it, My Father in heaven goes into action. And when two or three of you are together because of Me, you can be sure that I'll be there."

(Matthew 18:18-20 MSG)

What does it mean to take this most seriously? Jesus is saying that we should consider all He has said to the greatest extent. Take what He said to heart. Use it as we pray together. Remember what the Bible is saying to us. Touch and agree with your prayer partner. *"Again I say unto you, That if two of you shall agree on earth as touching any thing that they shall ask, it shall be done for them of my Father which is in heaven."* (Matthew 18:19) Find someone to agree with you via the telephone, in person, over the internet and/or through the mail. Find an Agree-er, and put God in remembrance of His Word. Stand on His promises, and watch them come to past in your lives. After you are freed from the snare of the enemy; walk into your season.

Chapter 6

"This is the day which the LORD hath made; we will rejoice and be glad in it." (Psalm 118:24)

This is your season; walk into it. God made this day for us, all of us. What are we going to do with it? We have been given so much but we are not using it. It is time. It is your time. Walk into your season of blessings, miracles, health, Ministry and all of the things God has given to you. What an honor and a privilege to be called a son and/or daughter of God. What an honor and a privilege to spread the Good News of Jesus Christ. It is indeed an honor and a privilege to live the abundant life in Christ on a daily basis. It is an honor and a privilege to be Children of The Reverend Clergy.

Just think, God chose you to be a part of the lineage to proclaim the message regarding His dear Son. He sees your heart and knows that He can use you and your family to bring souls into a saving knowledge of Jesus Christ. The ability to carry the weight of the anointing in and of itself is an awesome responsibility. It is also a humbling realization that God would trust someone like you with His creation. My brother, David, used to say "Shake it right off", when negativity came his way. Shake off the old unregenerate man with his deeds and be renewed in your mind by the Spirit of God. Ask God to give you clear direction. Allow Him to order your steps.

"The steps of a good man are ordered by the LORD: and He delighteth in his way." (Psalm 37:23)

Shake, shake, and shake it off of your heart, soul, spirit, mind and body. Fred Hammond sings a song called, "My Steps Are Ordered By God". God wants to order your steps. You must let Him. Give Him permission to guide and direct you in the affairs of life. Jesus promised never to leave you nor forsake you. God's promises are sure. What is promised in the Word of God is real. Make it real in your lives by applying them on a daily basis. Don't become obsessed with getting more material things. Be relaxed with what you have. *"Since God assured us, "I'll never let you down, never walk off and leave you," we can boldly quote, God is there, ready to help; I'm fearless no matter what. Who or what can get to me?"* (Hebrews 13:5-6 MSG) So, stop feeling sorry for yourselves. Stop the endless mind chatter. Trust in God.

E.M. Bounds wrote this statement: *"Trust is firm belief; it is faith in full bloom"*.

Accept the fact that God ordained both your Parents and your family. You cannot change that fact. You cannot change your DNA. You were not born into your family by mistake. It was by God's design. It is not a mistake that your Parents are members of The Reverend Clergy. Some are: Bishops, Pastors, Preachers, Rabbis, Priests, Evangelists, Missionaries, Deacons, etc. No, it is not a mistake that our Parents are labors, "together with God" of those who serve. You were chosen as constituents of the family of God. We are who we are by Divine appointment. You must suck it up and accept our family. You were fearfully and wonderfully made in the image and likeness of God our father. The blessings of your Parent(s) and my Parents are being passed on from generation to generation.

Do not resent God and the things of God. He loves you so much. He did not cause the pain and heartache you are experiencing. That is coming from the enemy of your soul. God want what is best for you and yours. He loves you with an everlasting love. He has drawn you with loving kindness unto Himself. Satan, the enemy of your soul use people to orchestrate situations and circumstances causing you to doubt the love of God.

Do not allow him to do such a thing. I encourage you to forget the past, and begin to dream again. Dare to dream. Dream big dreams. See yourself in your dream. Have a vision of your desired end. Remember: Without a vision the people perish. So, set goals, long term, and short term. Relentlessly pursue them. Go after them with a passion. Do not let anyone or anything deter you from reaching your desired end. Throw caution to the wind. It is time to get out of the boat. Walk on water and go to Jesus. You have been hurting for years, but this is your time. This is your season to soar like an eagle. I am reminded of a scripture that says:

"But they that wait upon the LORD shall renew their strength; they shall mount up with wings as eagles; they shall run, and not be weary; and they shall walk, and not faint."

(Isaiah 40:31)

You have been hindered for so long. The enemy has waged war on you. Didn't you know Jesus conquered death, hell and the grave? He gave all power into our hands. Satan is a defeated foe. I have a question to ask you. Did you know we won? Hallelujah! The battle is not your battle but it belongs to the LORD. I looked in the back of the book and we already won. When Jesus died on Calvary, He said: "It is finished." The work that He was sent to do has been completed.

Prodigal son, or daughter, you have wasted all of your inheritance. All of your money is gone. You would have eaten corncobs in the slop trough but no one would give them to you. Shake your self off. As you do, the blinders will come off your eyes and you will see that your father has more than enough for you. You will see how much your family loves and miss you. Dust yourself off and return home. What will it take for you to get up out of the hog pen? Will you come home? Swallow your pride and come home. No one is waiting to point a finger at you. They are waiting to love you past your dysfunction. They desire to love you in spite of your obvious hurts and pain. Take the sting out of it. Tell your loved ones that you thought you were right but you were wrong. Ask them to forgive you for all you have done to hurt the family.

Tell them you want to come home. You have come to yourself. Do not try to justify your wrong way of thinking any longer. It is not necessary. Get up now and go home.

Get up I said. Come out of the pigpen. Come out of it now. Stop eating the slop that was put in the hog trough. You have been in that hog pen far too long. You have wallowed in the mud far too long. Come home. Your family is waiting for you. While there is breath in your body, come home. Prodigal son and/or daughter, "It is time for you to come home where you belong". Get out of the mud. Come home where you belong. You have been sorely missed. Your family needs you to come home. They want you to come home. They love you. They realize you are hurting. They can feel your pain. Let them help you get through this pain. It is your restoration season. Repent. Do a 180 degree turn-around. Receive your total restoration in all things. It is yours. It is time to receive all that God has for you. God has liberated and set you free from the yoke of bondage. Stay free.

"If the Son therefore shall make you free, ye shall be free indeed."

(John 8:36)

Walk, live, move, breathe, bask in that freedom. It is yours for the taking. Stop making apologies for being born to Parents or a Parent in the Ministry. Stop making apologies for who you are and your inheritance. The devil has got to loose your belongings. Change your posture and position. You shall surely recover it all. Didn't you know that you are destined for greatness? There is nothing that you put your mind to do that you cannot accomplish. God has some wonderful things in store for you. Be proud that your Parents are working for the Almighty God, the Creator of the Universe. Rewards, in the Kingdom of God, surpasses any investment in a Success 1000 company in the world.

"And David enquired at the LORD, saying, Shall I pursue after this troop? Shall I overtake them? And he answered him, Pursue: for thou shalt surely overtake them, and without fail recover all."

(I Samuel 30:8)

28

Put your eyes on Jesus and keep them there. Be strong in the Lord and in the power of His might. Put on the whole armor of God that you might be able to stand against the wiles of the devil in the evil day. Take courage. Stop the whining. Quit whimpering. Don't be a jelly-back. Make the decision to change your posture and position. Rebuke indecision. Denounce all negativity. Stop the endless mind chatter. Do not let the devil control your mind. There is a battle going on for the minds of men. You have the victory in Christ Jesus. It is your victorious season. It is imperative that you search out and find the will of God for you. Get your thinking aligned with the Word of God. Straighten your life out. Don't confer with flesh and blood regarding it anymore. Seek God with all of your heart. Remember The LORD'S Prayer, Jesus said to His Disciples: *"When ye pray, say, Our Father which art in Heaven, Hallowed by Thy Name. Thy* Kingdom come. *Thy will be done, as in Heaven, so in earth. Give us this day our daily bread"*. That is the richest prayer. Heaven on earth is God's perfect will. So get your plan and purpose in life complete. Life is a journey, not a sprint. Micah presents this question to you.

"He hath shewed thee, O man, what is good; and what doth the LORD require of thee, but, to do justly, and to love mercy, and to walk humbly with thy God?"

(Micah 6:8)

Are you fulfilling God's requirement of you? God has shown you and told you in His Word what His requirements are. What are you doing with them? He wants you to be men and women of integrity in and out of the home. Humble yourselves in the natural and spiritual. This is a requirement from God. Jesus came meek and lowly, humble and Holy. It is very important to be merciful. Blessed are the merciful for they shall obtain mercy. Humility can take you to higher heights and deeper depths than you have ever known. Humbling yourselves before God means that you realize you were created to serve Him. You serve God also while serving those around you. If you are a Minister, your first responsibility is to serve others. God has opened many doors for you. Walk through the open doors. This is your season. Walk into it.

See yourself prosperous. See yourself in leadership positions. See yourselves as CEOs and CFOs of Success 1000 companies. See yourselves the head and not the tail in every situation. Donald Lawrence wrote a song called "Seasons". It encourages us to walk into our seasons of the positive seeds that we have sown. I encourage you to do the same. Be proactive; do not wait for something to happen. Make things happen for you. Seek after God for what you want with all diligence. Find your niche and pursue it. Never allow anyone to stop you from reaching your desired end.

Seasons by Donald Lawrence

"I know that you invested a lot
The return has been slow
You throw up your hands and say I give up
I just can't take it anymore.
But, I hear the Spirit say
That it's your time, the wait is over
Walk into your season
You survive the worst of times
God was always on your side
Stake your claim, write your name
Walk into this wealthy place.
The wait is over; it's your time
Walk into your season."

Be Aware of Hindrances

Chapter 7

The book of Nehemiah tells us a story of the Jews in Babylonian exile. Nehemiah was concerned for the welfare of Jerusalem and the inhabitants thereof. He desired to rebuild the walls of Jerusalem which was his homeland. It was in ruins. He wanted to protect the individuals that were still dwelling there.

Nehemiah's name in the Hebrew means "Comfort of Yahweh". He learns of the situation of his people. The affliction (distress), reproach of the people and the walls of Jerusalem that were broken down and the gates burned are explained in these chapters. Nehemiah intercedes with God. He puts a petition before King Artaxerxes and was granted permission to go assess the situation in Jerusalem. When he arrived at Jerusalem, the broken walls of the city were inspected. Nehemiah had his work cut out for him. He exhorted the people. After which, his enemies came up against him and he sent them an answer. He recorded everything that he did. He kept records of the builders. He was met with much opposition through threat of attack, discouragement, extortion, compromise, slander, treachery and was openly ridiculed. However, it did not stop him from completing the task that he was given; reconstructing the wall of Jerusalem.

Let's focus our attention on Chapter 6 verses 1-4. Nehemiah and his helpers were rebuilding the walls of Jerusalem. They were minding their own business. Although they were busy rebuilding the wall, their enemies were also busy trying to hinder the completion of this great project. When the wall had been complete but not the gates, Nehemiah received a false message requesting his presence in a bogus meeting. He declined the request. Verse 3 gives the response Nehemiah sent to his enemies. "I am doing a great work, so that I cannot come down; why should the work of the Lord cease, while I leave it, and come down to you?" Wouldn't you know that they were persistent in Verse 4 and sent unto him four additional times? His response was always the same.

There is nothing new under the sun. Rest assuredly; henchmen have been dispatched to hinder the Work that God has called you to do. They will use everything at their disposal to stop you in your tracks. He doesn't always show up looking, sounding and acting like the devil and his crowd. He comes as an angel of light. He will also use whomsoever he can to stop you. He will use those persons closest to you if they allow him to use them. The vessel he is operating in is not always an enemy. Sometimes it is a family member, friend and/or associate.

When your enemies come up against you to hinder your progress, what are you answering them? Are you leaving the call of God on your lives to answer your critics? Are you allowing your enemies to rule over you? Remember, Ephesians 6:12 affirms that you are *not* wrestling against flesh and blood, but against principalities and powers. The individuals are not your enemies. Your enemy is the evil spirit in back of them. What is the motivating force behind that person or situation? Check it out.

The sole purpose of your enemy is to keep you from advancing in the things of God. Realize this: He has declared war on God and His people. The devil desires to ascend above God, the throne of God and the people of God. God sometimes allow things to play out in our lives because we do not put a stop to it. God is in control of your life when you give it over to Him. That is the bottom line. The enemy is trying to destroy you. This is a fact that you cannot deny. You must become aware of this also. He wants you dead; of this you can be sure.

"Lest satan should get an advantage of us: for we are not ignorant of his devices."

(II Corinthians 2:11)

We are not ignorant of satan's devices. John 10:10, enumerates three: "The thief cometh not, but for to steal, and to kill, and to destroy," but Jesus came that we might have life, and have it more abundantly. Live your life to the fullest, let it overflow with joy. *"For the joy of the Lord is your strength.."* (Nehemiah 8:10d) The thief is a destroyer of homes; causes misery, murderer of babies, causes doubt, fear and unbelief, and is an accuser of the brethren. The enemy is speaking lies in the ears of individuals about you. They hate your guts, and despise you. You are not aware of it.

Some people in your home, church and family are carriers for the evil one. Recognize his deception. His primary aim is to get you out of the will of God. He will try to cause you to run ahead of God. He seeks to hurt God by hurting His creation. Don't get ahead of yourself; satan is a liar and the father of lies. Lies spoken consistently, if not checked, will become truth in the mind. Satan will use lies to try and deceive. God told us that, He *that worketh deceit shall not dwell within my house: he that telleth lies shall not tarry in my sight.* (Psalm 101:7) Some of these lies are believable. This is one of the reasons there is so much deception in the Houses of Worship. God said in the Bible that a liar would not tarry in His sight. Lying is listed in Proverbs 6:16-19 as one of the seven things the LORD hates. A lying tongue is the second thing mentioned on the list.

Do not allow liars to empty garbage into your spirit; make nests in your mind and/or heart. It is so important to cast down imaginations and every high thing that tries to exalt itself against the knowledge of God. It is time to pull down the satanic strongholds in your life and your family. Realize this: Jesus defeated satan on the Cross at Calvary more than 2000 years ago. Satan is a defeated foe, not going to be. He is a defeated foe now. Do not allow him to gain dominion over you and yours. The Bible states this truth to us: *"When the enemy comes up against you one way, the LORD will cause him to flee before you in seven different ways."* Trust God.

Be Watchful

First Peter 5:8 give the following warning: Be watchful. *"Be sober, be vigilant; because your adversary the devil, as a roaring lion, walketh about, seeking whom he may devour"*: Be aware of your surroundings. Do not walk around with blinders on. Take them off so that you can see. You also must have a clear head in this life. Do not live in a state of intoxication. Be serious and thoughtful in your demeanor and/or quality of life. An understanding of the facts, not speculation, should be your foundation. Know who you are and where you are going. When you know yourself and are secure in God, you can stand the test of time. Resist the devil. How do you resist him? You fight back with the Word of God. In Luke 4:4-10, when Jesus was tempted by the devil; Jesus gave him the Word of God. Take back what the devil has stolen from you through God's Son, Jesus Christ. Stop the mind chatter! You are not wrestling against flesh and blood according to Ephesians 6:12. What does it say? *"For we wrestle not against flesh and blood, but against principalities, against powers, against the rulers of the darkness of this world, against spiritual wickedness in high places."*

Satan is limited in what he can do. He doesn't know everything; God does. He is not everywhere present at the same time, but God is. God is the Creator. Satan is a created being. I encourage you to get to know the Creator for your self. When satan comes to trouble you, tell God about it. Continue seeking God until He intervenes on your behalf. Matthew 6:33 advises: *"But seek ye first the kingdom of God, and His righteousness; and all these things shall be added unto you"*. Satan cannot read your mind. So, cast down negative thoughts, recognizing they are not from God. James 4:7 enlightens us, *"Submit yourselves therefore to God. Resist the devil, and he will flee from you"*. Scripture says, Submit to God, Resist the devil, he will flee from us. It doesn't say, he might, nor perhaps. When we surrender to God; resist him, he *will* flee. Amen.

Know who you are in Christ Jesus. Do you really know who you are? Do you believe everything that you hear? Are you gullible? Vulnerable Christians are likely to believe almost anything they are told. They believe most Preachers. They tend to go everywhere to get hands laid on them. Someone told me a story about attending a Tent Meeting. She went down for prayer. The Preacher hit her head so hard, she could barely see. For hours, she wasn't able to drive. Friends took her to their home, nearby. They gave her pain medication and permitted her to rest. She is still "going down for prayer" shy. A beloved Mother, whose son was a Preacher, had an urgent need early one morning. She called several renown Prayer Ministries. Some asked, when she had last given to their work? One Ministry asked her if she were really saved? She called and called to no avail. She could not find anyone willing to agree with her in prayer that morning. Finally, she said, the Holy Spirit revealed to her: "You are calling all over the world looking for prayer, when I have given you your own son". She called her son. Half asleep, he prayed and agreed with his Mom. They are both in heaven now. Yet, it has been more than 25 years and God's answer to her prayer request is still standing firm. God is faithful.

Some are always looking for a word. Sometimes words are spoken from counterfeits such as *God told me to tell you*. Do you know that *these are dangerous words?* Satan comes as an angel of light. God told me. God told me. God told me this, that, or the other. God speaks to us through signs, wonders, people, the Bible, dreams, visions and in an audible voice. Be cognizant of this truth, that our only confirmation is the Word of God. *"God, who at sundry times and in divers manners spake in time past unto the fathers by the Prophets, Hath in these last days spoken unto us by His Son, whom He hath appointed heir of all things, by whom also He made the worlds;"* (Hebrews 1:2-3)

Watch and pray that you do not fall into temptation. Be sure you know who is laboring among you and yours. You should put your faith in Christ. It is time for you to know in whom you believe. The Bible tells us to be persuaded that He is able to keep everything that we have committed into His hands against that day. We are the righteousness of God in Christ Jesus. You must know who you are.

"Watch ye and pray, lest ye enter into temptation. The spirit truly is ready, but the flesh is weak." (Mark 14:38)

"THE BLESSING OF THE LORD,

IT MAKETH RICH, AND HE ADDETH

NO SORROW WITH IT."

Proverbs 10:22

Discovering Your Enemy

Chapter 8

Who is your enemy? Who has betrayed you? Why did you leave your comfort zone for a wilderness experience? This is a reality check! It was not and is not God, who was/is your enemy. Your loving and protective Heavenly Father is not your enemy. Your Clergy Parent(s) or guardian is not your enemy. Satan is the enemy of your soul.

"The thief cometh not, but for to steal, and to kill, and to destroy; I am come that they might have life, and that they might have it more abundantly." (John 10:10)

We are not ignorant of satan's devices. Three devices are illustrated here: They are to *steal* from you, *kill your dreams and desires,* and to ultimately *destroy* you. Jesus said, I am come that you might have and enjoy life to the fullest and until it overflows. Think about it, satan has three obliterating devices. These devices have destroyed thousands, if not millions of individuals, because they didn't use the Word of God. When in a spiritual struggle, or combat with the enemy, use God's Word. The Word of God will tear down satanic strongholds in your life and the lives of your loved ones.

Jesus was led into the wilderness to be tempted of the devil. When tempted, He quoted the Word of God to the devil. Jesus said, *"It is written. It is written. It is written."* When we are tempted and tried, it is essential that we follow our Savior's lead. Tell the enemy of your soul, *"It is written." God said it.* It is so. It will come to to pass. Expect it. What you had was stolen from you and your family by the enemy of your soul. He came to steal your birthright, your influence and your peace. He came to kill you and your influence. The attack is on. The weakest link in your armor is under attack. The object is to kill you and all those looking up to you.

Words Have Power

He wants to destroy you, your family, your reputation and ultimately your life. You are destroyed with the words of your own mouth. What are you saying? Words have creative power. *"For by thy words thou shalt be justified, and by thy words thou shall be condemned."* (Matthew 12:37) You can speak negative things into existence in your life. Your speech needs to change. Your attitude needs to change. You need to renew your mind with the Word of God. Stop saying things like, I almost laughed myself to death. I know this will not work. Stop speaking negative words over your lives. Your mind needs to be changed. You might say, "What do you mean, my mind needs to change?" If a man can control his mouth, he can control his entire body. You need a changed mind.

Romans 12:1-2, *"I beseech you therefore, brethren, by the mercies of God, that ye present your bodies a living sacrifice, holy, acceptable unto God, which is your reasonable service. And be not conformed to this world: but be ye transformed by the renewing of your mind, that ye may prove what is that good, and acceptable, and perfect, will of God".*

He who controls your mind will control your whole body. Who is controlling your mind? The scripture says: *"Let this mind be in you, which was also in Christ Jesus:"* (Philippians 2:5) *"This I say then, Walk in the Spirit, and ye shall not fulfill the lust of the flesh."* (Galatians 5:16) What does that mean? It means you have a choice. Let the mind of Christ be your mind, not some other mind. The choice is yours. Choose now this day who you will serve. Will you serve God or man? Will you allow God or the devil to control your mind, your flesh and your destiny?

"But He giveth more grace. Wherefore he saith, God resisteth the proud, but giveth grace unto the humble." (James 4:6)

"Likewise, ye younger, submit yourselves unto the elder. Yea, all of you be subject one to another, and be clothed with humility: for God resisteth the proud, and giveth grace to the humble." (I Peter 5:5)

"Love not the world, neither the things that are in the world. If any man love the world, the love of the Father is not in him. For all that is in the world, the lust of the flesh, and the lust of the eyes, and the pride of life, is not of the Father, but is of the world. And the world passeth away, and the lust thereof: but he that doeth the will of God abideth for ever." (I John 2:15-17)

"The fear of the LORD is to hate evil: pride, and arrogancy, and the evil way, and the froward mouth, do I hate." (Proverbs 8:13)

Make A Fresh Start

Find a fresh place to start over again. Make up your mind to change your posture and position. Let go of the bad and sometimes the good. Stop trying to bring your past into your future. Forget those things which are behind. It will not satisfy. You can't relive those years. Yesterday is gone. Stop living with regret. Getting rid of regret means you are making better choices. It comes to a point that it is just you and God. What are you doing with God? It is time to choose life. Stop saying I wish, I would have, should have, could have. Stop now and Live.

We make choices. Every choice we make affects our bloodline. The power of right choices is so amazing. Make the choice. God's arm is not short. He will pick you up out of the muck and miry clay. He will establish your comings and your goings because you are near and dear to Him. You must choose His love

39

and protection. Choose His guidance and direction. Choose to serve the True and Living God. He always provides new beginnings regardless of your situation. He knows what you need, when you aren't aware of your own need.

Jesus said, *"I AM that I AM." I AM here right now. Why are you afraid?* None of your weaknesses matter to God. Let God change your mess into your testimony, your ministry. God chooses the weak things of the world to confound the wise. Stop discounting yourself. Stop looking at your inadequacies. See God. Stop looking at the giants in the land. They have already been defeated. Just realize and know that God is greater than everything and everyone. Stop allowing your past to manipulate your present. Stop letting your present control your future. I dare you to give God your mess and watch Him make miracles out of it. True repentance leads to sweeping change. You can't tie Jesus into your messes. God has a perfect plan laid out for you in accordance to Ephesians 2:10 NASB: *"For we are His workmanship, created in Christ Jesus for good works, which God prepared beforehand so that we would walk in them."*

Stop right there. If you are not living for Jesus, you are miserable. It is time to get a fresh start. Get your heart in tuned with Jesus. Totally commit to Him. Experience a radical change in your lives, in your situations, family, and every facet of your lives. God has a great life in store for us. We must change our attitudes. Let go and let God. You need a fresh start. If you are resisting God in any area of your life, it will turn out badly for you.

God is the God of second chances, according to Isaiah 43:18-21. *"Remember ye not the former things; neither consider the things of old. Behold, I will do a new thing; now it shall spring forth; shall ye not know it? I will even make a way in the wilderness, and rivers in the desert. To give drink to My people, My chosen. This people have I formed for Myself; they shall shew forth My praise."* Forget about what has happened; don't keep going over old history. Be alert, be present. "I'm about to do something brand new. It's bursting out! Don't you see it? There it is! I'm making a road through the desert, rivers in the badlands for you. Wild animals will say, 'Thank you!' – coyotes and buzzards – Because I provided water in the desert, rivers through the sun-baked earth, Drinking water for the people I chose, the people I made especially for Myself, a people custom made to praise Me."

"Therefore if any man be in Christ, he is a new creature: old things are passed away: behold, all things are become new."

(II Corinthians 5:17)

Prayers for Deliverance and Salvation

God, I need you to change my heart. Make me new today. I want you to mold, shape and make me. Create in me a clean heart O God; renew the right spirit within me. Deliver me from blood guiltiness. O God. I want You to purge me thoroughly and sanctify me wholly, spirit, soul, mind and body. O LORD, open my lips; and my mouth shall show forth Your praise. I confess my need of total deliverance. Do it for me right now, LORD God. Thank you for hearing, and answering my prayer. I ask it in the Name of the LORD Jesus. It is done. Amen. Amen. (See Psalm 51:10-15)

God be merciful to me a sinner. I have sinned before God and man. I repent for all the wrong that I have done. I forsake my sin and all it offered. Jesus, come into my heart and become Lord and Master of my life. Live in me, LORD Jesus. Have Your way in my life. Wash me thoroughly from all my sins in Your Precious Blood. Take out my stony heart and give me a heart of flesh. I surrender all to You, LORD. Thanks for giving me the free gift of eternal life. I receive Jesus as LORD of my life. It is done in Jesus name. Amen. Amen. (See Luke 18:13)

Father, in the Name of Jesus, You said, "Come boldly before the Throne of Grace where we might find Mercy and Grace to help in the time of need". Father, here I am. I come before You, putting You in remembrance of Your Word Your Word declares

41

"Healing is the Children's bread". Another verse says "You sent Your Word and healed". Jeremiah 30:17a *reads "For I will restore health unto thee, and I will heal thee of thy wounds, saith the LORD".* Exodus 15:26e *affirms: "For I am the LORD that healeth thee".* You told us that the prayer of faith shall save the sick and You will raise them up. If they have committed any sin, it shall be forgiven. LORD, we believe Your Word. We apply Your Word to our lives on a daily basis. *"And ye shall serve the LORD thy God, and He shall bless thy bread, and thy water; and I will take sickness away from thy midst of thee."* (Exodus 23:25)

You also told me to put You in remembrance of Your Word. Your Son, Jesus Christ, took 39 stripes for my healing; I claim my healing right now. You told me that healing is the Children's bread. LORD, I am Your child. That means Jehovah-Rapha is my healer. He is my doctor in a sick room, lawyer in a courtroom. Let your healing virtue flow throughout my body from the crown of my head to the very souls of my feet in the name of Jesus. It is done. Amen.

Chapter 9

Hey you. Are you talking to me? Yes, you. Preachers' Kids, also known as PKs. We need to talk. Talk? What do you mean talk? Let's talk now. What are we going to talk about? Let's discuss your life as a PK. We need to talk about challenges to *LIVING IN A GLASS HOUSE; LIVING IN A BUBBLE; AND LIFE UNDER A MICROSCOPE. What is it like* living with *Paparazzi* following you around. It is important. Let's talk.

Your Parent(s) may be a Bishop, Minister, Pastor, Evangelist, Missionary, Rabbi, Priest, Prophet, Prophetess, Teacher, Deacon, etc. Their lives are on display, up for public scrutiny, but not yours. The lives of your Parents are open books. You are having issues sharing your Cleric Parent(s) with the public and their involvement. You may wish to share your life experiences with an individual(s) of your choice.

People are watching your every move. You cannot go anyplace and/or do anything without someone watching you and/or eavesdropping on your conversation. You are yelling internally; leave me alone. My life is not an open book. My Dad and Mom's lives were open books. However, not mine. I want to be a normal person. I want to play, laugh, and make merry with my friends. I want to run and jump. I want to play sports. I want to go shopping. I want to dress down. My Parent(s) and/or guardian(s) are Ministers, not me. Leave me alone. Let me live my life. Stop comparing me with your Children.

You are being compared with the Children of the laity. Non-Preachers' Kids can do whatever they want when they want. They drink, smoke, curse, party and do all kinds of things, but nothing is said. They are watching every step a Preachers' Kids make. We are expected to be perfect because of our Minister Parent(s). If there are flaws in our lives, then their Children are off the hook. They are told from childhood, if the Preachers' Kids aren't perfect how we can expect perfection from our children. Non-Preachers Kids are told, "Do the best you can." They live with the Preacher and live ragged lives. Go on with your lives. Sow your wild oats. Whatever you can do just do it. You are a child of the laity. It is okay if you act unseemly but not the Preachers' Kids.

As a PK, if you sneeze wrong, it is held against you. If you laugh out loud, there is an issue. Your clothes have issues. Everything you do is wrong. You are told that you will never measure up to their kids. You will never be anything. "*Preachers' Kids Are The Worst Kind.*" It is time to nip this garbage in the bud. People are jealous of you and your family. They want the name recognition you have. God has called your family into Ministry. All Preachers' Kids are called into some kind of Ministry. Some into the pulpit, some into street Ministry, some into the music Ministry, some Social Services, some into fundraising Ministry, some teachers, some prayer warriors, some maintenance, some prison Ministry, some addiction Ministry, some hospitality, some kitchen Ministry, some Missionaries, some Children's Ministry, some administration, some healthcare, some legal, some education, and some are ushers and greeters, etc. Wherever God plants you and whatever is needed is Ministry. Come as you are, and let God make you what He wants you to be.

"For we are laborers together with God: ye are God's husbandry, ye are God's building." (I Corinthians 3:9)

Who are you? Why are you here? How can I expect to go back to who I was before the hurt? You are a Preachers' Kids. You are here as an extension of God's arms to Minister to the needs of mankind. We all have a calling on our lives. We need to find the real role. Who are you really? Why are you here? Find excitement and passion in the process of who you are. My Dad taught us that no one is better than you. You are as good as or better than anyone walking on two feet. Take your life back. Delete all negative messages. Mark them: *"Return to sender. Addressee unknown."*

Reject all negative messages regardless of the sender. One part of the whole armor of God is the Shield of Faith where you are able to quench the fiery darts of the wicked. The fiery darts of the wicked are words. The book of James in the Bible talks about the tongue being an unruly member that we use to bless God and curse men. The tongue is full of deadly poisons a world of iniquity. Proverbs says a man is snared by the words of his mouth. Watch what you say. The world was made by God's Words. God created the world with the power of His Words. In the book of Genesis chapter one, the scripture says that He said, He said, He said several times. Then the scripture said, He saw what He said. We have the same power in our words. Job said, *"Thou shall also decree a thing, and it shall be established unto thee. And the light shall shine upon thy ways."* (Job 22:28)

There is power in words. *By your words you are justified and by your words you are condemned.* (Matthew 12:37) *Death and life are in the power of your tongue* (your words). (Proverbs 18:21 AMP) Words have creative power, especially, the words spoken after I am. *I AM* are two of the most powerful words in the English language. You can speak good or bad things into existence using *I AM*. These two words can shape or break an individual's life. Direct each word before you say or write it behind *I AM*.

Examples of The Potency of I AM:

Moses asked God who should I say sent me? God's answer was I AM that I AM. I AM the Self-Existent One, The Eternal, The One Who Always Has Been And Always Will Be. This is shortened to I AM Here, The Ever-Present and Living One. It is equivalent to GOD, The Eternal.

45

Cassius Clay, also known as: Mohammed Ali, proclaimed many years ago, *I AM The Greatest*. During his entire boxing career, he remained *The Greatest*. Today, to most Americans, he still is seen as *The Greatest.*

Stop Trying To Please Man

Sometime ago, I heard this story. The truth and the lie were taking a bath. Lie finished first and dried off, putting on the truths clothing. People saw him walking down the street and said, "There is the lie dressed up like the truth." The truth dried off; saw the lie's clothing, and refused to put them on. He decided to walk down the street with no clothes. People saw him and said, "There is the naked truth." God said in Psalm 101, that a liar would not tarry in His sight.

Ask the Lord to deliver you from people. Please God not man. Man will let you down. Man will anesthetize you. Do not allow man to talk you out of your inheritance. Realize that persecution occurs at various levels in our lives and strikes from a variety of sources. Did you know that regrets, guilt, and remorse can torture the soul? Choose to take a positive attitude toward persecution. Every man, woman, boy or girl must take a stand for what he believes and run the risk of rejection and/or ridicule.

Forgive those who have hurt you. Ask God for His Divine intervention. Jesus said, *"Father, forgive them for they know not what they do."* Trust God to do what you ask of Him. Allow Him to turn persecution into opportunities for showing compassion, caring for the sick, forgiveness, etc. Let me explain. You were created in the image and likeness of God. When you ask someone if they are having a good day and they respond no. Remind them to appreciate and value what they have. You can see that they have the activity of their limbs. Nonetheless, they seem to be saying to God, although I am physically fine, it isn't enough. Ask yourself how often do we seem to disregard the blessings of the LORD. *"This is the day that the LORD has made. We will rejoice and be glad in it."* Are you rejoicing? Who or what has stolen your joy?

46

Let your past go. Stop living in the past. Philippians 3:13-14 gives us a simple directive. *"Brethren, I count not myself to have apprehended: but this one thing I do, forgetting those things which are behind, and reaching forth unto those things which are before, I Press toward the mark for the prize for the high calling of God in Christ Jesus."* God has a plan for your life. Renew your mind and thoughts with the Word of God. Remember, "As a man thinks in his heart so is he". Speak words out of your mouth that line up with the Word of God. God and His Word are inseparable. Declare His Word in season and out of season. Eat sleep and drink the Word of God. "It is a lamp unto your feet and a light unto your pathway." Decree and declare, who you are, in accordant to the Word of God.

You Are A King's Kid

Do you know who you are? You are a King's Kid. You are made in the image, and likeness of Almighty God. He is your righteousness. You are fearfully and wonderfully made. You are anointed with the burden removing, yoke destroying power of Almighty God. He is in control of every facet of your life. You have such an anointing on your life. God is always there in the personage of the Holy Spirit walking you through every situation. Although you are "L*iving In A Glass House*," put your trust in God.

Jesus promised never to leave you nor forsake you. He promised to be with us until the end of the world. I am so glad about it. Aren't you? I want to encourage you to put your *"Trust in the Lord with all your heart. Lean not unto your own understanding, In all of your ways acknowledge Him and He shall direct your path".* (Proverbs 3:5-6 AMP) It takes one word from God to change your situation. It takes one word from God to change you in the midst of your situation. Nothing you do can replace the time you spend alone with God. Take the limits off of Him.

You must renew your mind with the Word of God. His Word is a lamp unto your feet and a light unto your pathway. Get away from feeling sorry for yourself. Woe is me for I am undone should not be a part of your life. Poor me, nothing is ever going right for me. Remove from your mindset. Everybody is against me.

47

There is nothing I can do to change my plight. I encourage you to stay away from every evil thought. Stop feeling sorrow for yourself. You need to eat, sleep, and live. *"Cast down imaginations and every high thing that exalts itself against the knowledge of God. Bring every thought into captivity to the obedience of Christ."*

(II Corinthians 10:5)

Stop the endless mind chatter. Begin to release words out of your mouth that will establish who you are in Christ Jesus. Speak the Word of God with wisdom, boldness and authority. The words that you speak are spirit and life. Watch what you say out of your mouth. Meditate upon the living Word of God. Do the Word on a daily basis. Plant it in your heart that you might not sin against God. Always study the Word. Begin the process of seedtime, and harvest. Get involved in seedtime, and harvest. Pray in the Spirit for clear concise directions. *"Build yourself up on your most holy faith, praying in the Holy Ghost."* (Jude 20)

Plant Righteous Seeds

Remain consistently committed to what you plant and walk in it. Expect to reap a bountiful harvest on the seed that you sow. My Mom always told us that we would reap what we sow. Take a principle; operate in it consistently to receive a breakthrough. That principle is found in Galatians 6:7. *"God is not mocked: for whatsoever a man soweth that shall he also reap."* When you sow seed, it will produce a bountiful harvest. When bad or good seed is sown, you will reap that harvest. If you desire a breakthrough in your life, work the principle until something positive materializes for you. If things are happening in your life that is not a result of seeds you have sown, tell that devil, "I didn't sow these seeds, and I am not going to reap this harvest." You do not have to receive everything the devil throws your way. Resist the devil and he will flee from you. Resist him by not following his tactics.

Delight yourself in the things of God. Be pliable, flexible, workable, obedient and loyal. Loyalty is changing your plans to accommodate someone else. How often do you change your plans to help someone other than yourself? When your heart is pliable, God can come in and direct His Will and Way in your heart. You can't stop an individual who knows that His God is with him. Put that individual in any situation and he will succeed.

"For they being ignorant of God's righteousness, and going about to establish their own righteousness, have not submitted themselves unto the righteousness of God." (Romans 10:3)

"For I say, through the grace given unto me, to every man that is among you, not to think of himself more highly than he ought to think; but to think soberly, according as God hath dealt to every man the measure of faith." (Romans 12:3)

"Therefore let no man glory in men; for all things are yours;"
(I Corinthians 3:21)

"For who maketh thee to differ from another? and what hast thou that thou didst not receive? now if thou didst receive it, why dost thou glory, as if thou hadst not received it."
(I Corinthians 4:7)

"Casting down imaginations, and every high thing that exalteth itself against the knowledge of God, and bringing into captivity every thought to the obedience of Christ."
(II Corinthians 10:5)

"Let nothing be done through strife or vainglory; but in lowliness of mind let each esteem other better than themselves."
(Philippians 2:3)

"Whose end is destruction, whose God is their belly, and whose glory is in their shame, who mind earthly things."
(Philippians 3:19)

"Not a novice, lest being lifted up with pride he fall into the condemnation of the devil." (I Timothy 3:6)

"For men shall be lovers of their own selves, covetous, boasters, proud, blasphemers, disobedient to parents, unthankful, unholy."
(II Timothy 3:2)

"Every good gift and every perfect gift is from above, and cometh down from the Father of lights, with whom is no variableness, neither shadow of turning." (James 1:17)

"But if ye have respect to persons, ye commit sin, and are convinced of the law as transgressors." (James 2:9)

50

Chapter 10

Preachers' Kids, realize before you can complete anything you start, it requires commitment. How committed are you? Do you start multiple tasks, and do not finish them? How many uncompleted task do you have on your plate at this time? Are you committed to the very end? I encourage you to go all the way with the LORD. Set your face like a flint until you reach the end of the road. Prove God and watch Him come through for you and yours. You ask yourselves, "How can this thing work for me? What if I commit and fail?" Yes, it can and will work for you. Nothing beats a failure, but a try. Step out on the water and go to Jesus. It is time to get out of your comfort zone.

Stop retaking the chapter test. It is time for the mid-term and then the final. Speak life in your dry and dying places. Death and life are in the power of your own tongue. Choose to speak life. Decree the Word of God like Job. *"Thou shalt also decree a thing, and it shall be established unto thee: and the light shall shine upon thy ways."* (Job 22:28) What you decree shall be established, not might, perhaps or maybe. When you make your decree, *light shall shine* upon your path. What are you decreeing in your life today?

Do not back up, give up, cave in and/or quit. When you do, you doubt the truth of God's Word. Take God at His Word. Decree and declare in the name of Jesus, I am victorious. I can do all things through Christ who strengthens me. The song said, *In the name of Jesus, I have the victory and demons have to flee.* You experience victory when you stand on the Word of God from Genesis to

Revelation. Stand on the Promises of God. Remind God of what He said in His Word and He will bring it to pass. You have got to know that this thing works. If it doesn't work, you need to go on to something else. Aren't you glad to know that there are no flaws in the things of God? You cannot find any discrepancies. God's Word works all by itself.

I am here to tell you that it works. Just take a stand for right and righteousness. *"My God shall supply all your need according to His riches in glory by Christ Jesus."* (Philippians 4:19) Tenacity must rise up in you. Always know that God can and will supply all your needs. If you are to doubt anything, doubt your doubts not God. How do you know what God can and will do? The answer can be found in the Word of God. Search the Scriptures daily for in them you have life and they do testify of the Authenticity and Divinity of our Lord and Savior Jesus Christ. Deposit on the inside of you the experience of victorious living. As you study the Bible, question if you have deposited that experience within your heart, soul, mind, body and spirit. Meditate on the Word of God. Think deep on God's Word. Dissect the Word of God. Analyze the Word. Apply God's Word. Get a promise from the Bible and stand on it. God's Word is forever settled in heaven. It is alive. It is quick, powerful and sharper than a two-edged sword. It goes directly to the root cause of your issues when it is applied. God's Word is good for what ails you, physically, mentally, emotionally, socially, financially, and even materially.

The more incompletes you have, the more questions and doubts consume you. You will experience having burdens removed and yokes destroyed because of the anointing as you become saturated in God and His Word is in you. The Holy Spirit is telling you to go ahead, step out on the water and go to Jesus. When you do this, nothing shall be impossible for you. Jesus was committed to die on the cross for you and me. He would not be deterred. He was committed to realizing the resurrection experience. Be encouraged to stay committed to God and His Word. Keep going. Do not stop. No matter what you hear, keep going. Do not allow negativity to stop you from reaching your desired end. Jealous people are on the bottom trying to bring you down to their level. Do not let that happen.

God wants to get you into a place where He can speak to you. He is committed to you. Seek His face. God desires intimacy with you. Learn who your Heavenly Father is. Get a personal relationship with Him through our Lord and Savior Jesus Christ. God is in love with you. Let me say that again. *God is in love with you.* He hates your sin but He loves you so every much. Stop lying on God. He is not punishing you. His presence can't indwell you or come upon you when you are practicing and living in sin. Accept Jesus as Lord; and make a commitment to serve Him.

All God wants from you is YOU. Take care of the body God has given you. He is standing with His arms wide open asking you to come into His presence. *"Behold, I stand at the door and knock. If any man hear My voice and open up to Me, I will come into Him and sup with him and He with me."* (Revelations 3:20) What bothers you, bothers Him. Do not push Him away from you. He desires to be involved in every facet of your life. God is saying, *"Come to Me; I will give you rest."* You can find rest in the presence of Almighty God. In His presence is fullness of joy and at His right hand are treasures forever more. You can cease from all of your toiling.

Restoration

Is there anything missing in your life? This is your day of restoration. You can be restored back to your place in God. Trust Him. God loves you so much with an everlasting love. He has drawn you unto Himself with loving kindness. In God's presence, the restoration process can be completed. What is restoration? Restoration is putting back what was missing in your life. It is a return, total restitution. The Winans sang a song years ago that says *Restoration has finally come. I have been restored BACK to my place in God.* The day of total restoration is here for you. Rejoice.

This is your *Restoration Day*. When I think of restoration, I think of the prodigal son in Luke 15:11-32 and his return home from another country in the hog pen. His father received him home; gave him a ring of gold; put him on a robe; killed the fatted calf and gave him something he didn't ask for on that day.

The prodigal son decided he wanted all of his inheritance. His father gave him his portion and off he went. He spent all of his inheritance on riotous living. This young man ended up in the hog pen. He was eating the corn hulks from the hogs when he came to himself. O' what a restoration day that was for the prodigal son and his family. When his father saw him coming down the road, things began to change in that household. He immediately had a celebration because the son that he thought was gone had come back home. It was total restoration back to his place in the family. He was pleased that the son who was lost returned home. God is like the father of the prodigal son. He wants to restore you back to your place in Him. God gave us a promise in Joel 2:25, *"And I will restore to you the years that the locust hath eaten, the cankerworm, and the caterpillar, and the palmerworm, my great army which I sent among you."* God gave us many good and precious promises in His Word. God and His Word are inseparable.

Your restoration day is the day the LORD is rolling away the shame and disgrace of your past. He is waiting for you to return home. You left home. Will you come home today? It is easy to do. Just repeat this prayer with me. God be merciful to me, a sinner. Forgive me for my sins. Wash me in the Blood of the Lord Jesus Christ. Save my soul and write my name in the Lamb's Book of Life. I ask it in the Name of Jesus. Amen.

Chapter 11

Mother Mary Ruth Bowens Story
(My Mom at 90 years young)

Dealing with Peers

My Mom's Dad was a Preacher. She was the oldest of five Children. Mom's peers compared their parents with Mom's Parents. They were envious of her and would take things from her, such as her lunch. Lunch would consist of meat, peas or beans, cake or pie in a tin pail. After they ate her lunch, they would laugh saying, "I am full". Her friends would say, "Oh, she is a good person. She won't do anything bad to any of you although you ate her lunch". They would poke fun at her because her father was a Minister and she didn't wear pants.

Question: While growing up, did you resent God, and/or the Church?

Answer: No. I received the Holy Ghost in the middle of a cotton field in the heat of the day. I went down to the Mercy Seat one day and the Holy Ghost came. That very day, I was filled with the Holy Ghost. I don't have a care in the world. I have cast all my cares on the LORD knowing He cares for me.

Words of Wisdom:
Mother Mary Ruth Bowens

During her life, she became an ardent Author,
Preacher/Teacher and Radio Co-Pastor.

Mom's Story

I was nineteen years old when I married my late husband, Bishop George Law Bowens, Jr. I never talked back to my Parents. My Mom taught us, a smile will carry you a long way. I was an honor student in school and I won many Spelling Bees. Although I didn't finish high school, God blessed me abundantly. I knew more than my peers who graduated. They did not understand it. But, I was always reading, and writing. My Parents took me out of school to help with my siblings, and chores on the farm. Older children were always expected to help with everyday tasks and farm duties. I wasn't bitter. I did what was required of me. My mind was continually stimulated, because I loved to read. I would read the Word of God, as well as other books and the newspaper, all of the time. In God's Word, the Bible, I found wisdom, knowledge and understanding. The Bible says, *"If any of you lack wisdom, let him ask of God, that giveth to all men liberally, and upbraided not; and it shall be given him"*. (James 1:5) God will give you what you are in the need of. God always gives work; but not everyone has the same job.

I encourage you to repent for all of the wrongs you have done. Ask God to forgive you for your sins. Invite Jesus to come into your heart and become LORD and MASTER of your life. Take a 180 degree turn, not a 360 degree. A 360 degree turn means you have gone around in a circle. A 180 degree means you have changed your posture and position. You have dealt with the sin and decided to give up all to follow Jesus. Do yourself a favor and stop telling people your dreams and your secrets. They will envy you and try to hinder your receiving the blessing of the LORD that make rich and

He adds no sorrow with it. Talk to them about your realities. Tell them that you were once on skid row, but God. You were a wretch undone, but God. You were too mean to live, and afraid to die, but God. You once were lost but God. Now you are found. You were blind but God. Now you can see! Hallelujah.

James' Story

You should always be straight with every individual. Each person has a mind of his or her own. Even if they deviate because of training, they will come back. Being taught the right way kept me from trouble. When things were out of the ordinary, I fled from it. Something serious can happen if you hang around undesirables. Honor your Parents. Respect adults and you will go far in life. Always listen to sound advice. It will help you. When you have good parents, members of The Reverend Clergy, or not; and if you are taught the right way of life, even when you have aged, it will stay with you. Good training: when you are taught right from wrong – you have just as many rights, regardless of status.

Christian Children and Preachers' Kids should all be good Children, because you come from a good home. If he or she is training their Children according to God's standards, there should be no difference. All of us are Ministers one to another. When you get up and testify, you are Ministering to somebody. Jesus told us in the Great Commission, Mark 16:15, *"And He said unto them, Go ye into all the world, and preach the Gospel to every creature"*. This mandate was given to every man, woman, boy and girl.

"For we have not an High Priest which cannot be touched with the feeling of our infirmities; but was in all points tempted like as we are, yet without sin." (Hebrews 4:15) We are not angels, who are not tempted. Jesus was tempted in all things, as we are, but He did not sin. We are Children of the King; the same as other Children whose Parents happen to be Ministers. Preachers' Kids are Kids regardless of their Parent's status. We all must accept Jesus the

same: as all men, women, boys and girls. Jesus made a life-giving blood sacrifice for all mankind. The status of your Parents has nothing to do with your personal relationship with Him. As the Great Commission advises in Mark 16:16: *"He that believeth and is baptized shall be saved; but he that believeth not shall be damned"*. Now you are thinking how can a good God allow His Children to be damned. Your finale, nor my end result is not in God's hand. Rather repentance is in our hands. Paul said in Acts 16:31, *"Believe on the Lord Jesus Christ, and thou shall be saved, and thy house"*. *"(For He saith, I HAVE HEARD THEE IN A TIME ACCEPTED, AND IN THE DAY OF SALVATION HAVE I SUCCOURED THEE: behold, now is the accepted time; behold, now is the day of salvation)."* (II Corinthians 6:2)

Helen's Story

Externals didn't affect me as much as what my Dad would say and do. The main things that inspired me were, my Dad was a leader, and a very strong man. I thank God for having my Dad because of who he was. I am the woman I am today, because of my Parents.

Dad spent extra time with us no matter what he did outside the home. Mom held things together while Dad was out. Mom was a strong woman, full of love and compassion. Sometimes I would get jealous, because so many people would come around her and take up her time. Our home life would make up for what went on outside. I choose to see the positive side, and let go and let God.

Jesus passed the torch to His disciples. The disciples passed the torch to the people and the people to each other from generation to generation. Dad and Mom passed the torch to us (their Children). We are to live right before our Children and pass it on to them. We are praying that their Children will honor their Grandparent's legacy and pass it on to future generations. Let's keep passing the torch, from generation to generation, to the Glory of God.

Dad was a very strong and wise man with a meek and quite spirit who always took up time with me. If anything negative were said, I would let it pass over me. I was taught to refuse to pick up the negative. Dad would call us his Gals. That term of endearment made us feel so very special. We felt like Princesses. That was one of many bright spots in our lives. He was a very positive image to his children, and the world. He held up the torch (Jesus is the light of the world), everywhere he went. I thank the LORD for being a Preachers' Kid. I was told this, "You think you are something because your father is a Preacher". My response was, "I am something". Long before Dad became a Bishop, he was a man's man, not a jelly-back. He was a genuine man of God. Dad was not a whoremonger. He was a man after God's own heart.

Preachers' Kids were not ridiculed until parents started to talk about the Preacher and his family in front of their Children at home. People started to reject God becoming indifferent to Him and His Word. Trust and respect for one another started to dwindle. When I grew up, Dad was a Sharecropper. We lived in a controlled environment. I was not exposed to a lot of negativity. I thank God for that.

Many of our parents are not practicing what they are Preaching. Realizing there is so much sexual promiscuity in the Church/Temple/Synagogue, as well as other Houses of Worship among the Ministerial Cleric. When you turn on the news, it is commonly reported that Pastors, Rabbis, Priests, and other members of The Reverend Clergy are caught up in the lusts of their flesh, and the pride of life. These scandalous situations are causing so much pain, and embarrassment not only to the Body of Christ, but to their individual families. When their sin(s) have been exposed to the world, the children are made a mockery. They are ridiculed, picked at, and made fun of.

59

Maudesta's Story

I hated every moment of my life as a Preachers' Kid. The Church people took all of our time from our parents. We were taught to live godly lives in Church, but we felt that no love was shown to us at the home. LOVE was Preached in the Church, but seldom demonstrated at home. I felt my Parents were living a lie, and I wanted no part of it. I refused to be manipulated by them, but the LORD made up for it all.

God was constantly being questioned by me. God, if You are LOVE and my parents are Your representatives on this earth, where is the LOVE? It seems to me that they forgot You called them to be Parents to their own Children, first. The first thing the Lord gave them was parenting. In those days, you were not allowed to say how you felt about anything. I thought my Parents were phonies because they talked LOVE but did not always appear to show LOVE to their own Children. My Parents pretended everything was fine at home, but it was not. I always voiced my opinion, and was called the black sheep of the family. I was always rebellious about the status quo.

I was called PK or Ms. Holier-than-Thou very often. No one wanted to play with me because I was so 'churchy'. There was a lot of ridicule. There are many devils out there to try and make you run away from God and the things of God. Although that happened, I was protected by God. Satan and his imps will try to make you cry, and make you wish you were not a PK, especially if you are saved. All of these things made me very angry.

If anyone knocked the chips off of my shoulder, that would be their behinds. I would fight. I was very bitter. Jealousy, envy, strife, and hatred of others abided with me until salvation. That is when the LORD changed me. I would fight anybody, whether they were talking to me, or someone else. "LORD, show me your LOVE was my constant cry." He showed me that I am the object of His LOVE. With His loving kindness, God drew me unto Himself.

60

I asked God directly to show me His LOVE. I questioned Him as to what was going on in my life as an adult, and what I should do? He showed me directly. After that time, I learned many lessons. He taught me to become Christ-like. Be firm; say no, and mean it. Make decisions, and stick to them. Do not argue with anyone about your choices. Listen to God regarding His plans for your life. He will work it out for you. God sees not as the world sees. Make right choices for yourselves. God will let you know when you go wrong. The Holy Spirit will check you every time. For years, I had feelings of rejection; over time, God healed my emotions.

The Word of God saturated me, took things apart, and showed me the things I needed to get rid of. My Parents had seven Children. During my rebellion, Dad advised my siblings to leave me alone. Dad would tell them, when God gets through with her, you will be surprised at the outcome. I was 27 years old when I accepted Jesus as LORD. The only thing that God gave me was an over-abundance of LOVE. His LOVE is more than enough. It was what I desired most in this world, LOVE. When I got that in my head and heart, it brought about a change in me.

When my sin started to turn inside, I would go to the club where I loved to dance. I could dance really well. One night in the club, the LORD put an invisible lasso around my legs and I couldn't dance any more. I became internally miserable until I grew weary. I cried out to the LORD, "My Parents can't do it, but if you want me, here I am." "*As the hart panteth after the water brooks, so panteth my soul after Thee, O God.*" (Psalm 42:1) For ten continuous years, God worked on me. After being away from home for years, God finally permitted me to go home. He affirmed His LOVE in my life to my family. As an old song goes, "O' O' O' what He has done for me, I never shall forget what He has done for me". My family could hardly believe the change in my life. What God has done for me is phenomenon. Yet, my dear friends, "It is no secret what God will do, what He has done for others, He will do for you".

Let me regress for a minute. I became pregnant at age 17. My Mom did not take me to a Doctor. Instead, she took me to a Home for Unwed Mothers in New York. My Dad did not try to stop her. Dad allowed my Mom to put me out. You want me to believe, that God through the Holy Spirit is using them to Minister to the masses, the LOVE of God. They cannot express that LOVE to their own Children?

God was constantly showing me how much He LOVES me. He has given me His LOVE, joy, peace, goodness and mercy. He taught me this fact and I am holding onto it. Jesus promised that He would never leave me nor forsake me. I know now, that nothing can separate me from the LOVE of God. *"Who shall separate us from the love of Christ? Shall tribulation, or distress, or persecution, or famine, or nakedness, or peril, or sword?"* (Romans 8:35) Jesus took that little bit of faith I had, and poured His LOVE through the Holy Spirit all over it. That is why I do not understand why people do not LOVE the LORD. Psalm 34:8 says, *"O taste and see that the LORD is good: blessed is the man that trusteth in Him"*.

Preachers' Kids, you walked away from your home and family because you were fed up. You didn't want any part of God, family nor the things of God. You are tired of sharing your Parents with the masses. You are also tired living under scrutiny, in a glass bubble. You are tired of the God-thing. You are tired of pretentious folk. Is this all there is to life and the world? There must be something else? Where is the LOVE? These people talk LOVE all the time, but do not live it.

All I ever hear in Church is the LOVE of God. How much people feel LOVE in the church is always spoken of. I have felt the LOVE of God in some Churches, but not all of them. As a child, you are not aware of the differences and what they are. Some Churches are full of legalism. While others have a form of godliness, but denying the power thereof. Some Churches have the presence of God in its fullness, Yet, in others the Glory of the LORD has departed from those places. Nonetheless, they are going on anyway.

When God delivers you, it is not totally for you only. Allow your life to become a living testimony for others. God blessed you to make you a blessing. Someone may hear your testimony and turn to the LORD Jesus Christ for salvation. Hallelujah. You do not need to stoop to that individual's level to bring them up to your level. This is the day of repentance. You may fall many times, but make up your mind that you will not quit. It is easy to go back to what you are accustomed to, rather than pressing forward to a higher calling in Christ Jesus. God promises restoration. Joel 2:25-26 reads: *"And I will restore to you the years that the locust hath eaten, the cankerworm, and the caterpillar, and the palmerworm, My great army which I sent among you. And you shall eat in plenty, and be satisfied, and praise the Name of the LORD your God, that hath dealt wondrously with you: and My people shall never be ashamed"*. Separation from the world through consecrated prayer and fasting, helps to yield spiritual growth. The anointing is needed to remove burdens and destroy the yoke of the enemy.

Janice's Story

I am a daughter of a Pastor. My Parents loved us and cared for us. They took care of us and provided for us in every facet of our lives. My Dad and Mom were godly examples inside and outside of the home. We always went on family vacations and enjoyed the holidays together. When we took vacations together, I was excited because we would get to know each other all over again. I felt very secure in my Parents love. They did what they knew to do, based upon their experiences. As long as they were providing, they were demonstrating their love and support.

While I was attending Vacation Bible School, between the ages of nine and twelve years old, two teachers reprimanded me. They made a big deal over having to chastise me, because I was doing what children do – talking with my friends. They really carried on about my Dad being the Pastor. I guess they called themselves making an example of me. Upon reaching adulthood, I realized how much people try to take certain liberties with you. They think they can say anything to you. I had to correct them and let them know, I am on equal grounds with you.

After I gave birth to my first child, people attacked me because of my weight gain. At that time I began to come out of myself. As I went through changes with Church people, I began to speak up. They sometimes tried to put their feelings off on me. I gained self-confidence. When I have a conviction, I speak up now. It didn't make sense to me what they did. I did not have a behavior problem. My Parents instilled certain values and attitudes. I trusted people and tried to get along well with everyone.

Many times different ones would come to our home. It was fun having visitors. It didn't interfere with my childhood. My siblings and I always had company. Our Parents would sometimes allow us to walk home with friends. People say that *Preachers' Kids are the worst kind*. I didn't like the stereotype that was being put upon me. They didn't have the place to say such a thing. We live in a fish bowl. Everything we do and did was magnified 1000 times over. Their statement put pressure on me to prove them wrong. People liked me because I was the Pastor's daughter. Some disliked me for the same reason.

Preachers' Kids, perhaps you have allowed people to hinder your growth and development. Stop letting others determine your vocational choices. Do not sell yourself short. Never under estimate yourself. You can reach your goals. Learn to know God for yourself. It is not based upon anyone but you. Know who you are in Christ. He loves you unconditionally. You do not have to allow people to dictate to you. If people cannot accept you, that is their issue. Do not let them put you through changes. Some have ulterior motives. They will have you going through mental and emotional changes. God loves you. He knows you are His child.

People will try to put pressure on you. They will toss you to the side, if they cannot use you for their own purposes. Sometimes you feel pressure because of their expectation of you. All of us have certain gifts. Know what God has given you. Be secure in God's love. You do not need people's approval. You have been accepted by God. Never feel pressure to please everyone. Know in your knower, that God is always there to keep you from all hurt, harm and danger.

Carolyn's Story

Preachers' Kids are the most significant of Church people; both in and out of Church venues. If we are in it, it is 100%. The biggest thing in the world is Church to PKs. If we live through Church and make a determination to follow Jesus, we are in it for the long haul. You also know how to fake it. You know all the movements. When you are fixed in serving Jesus, you will not be moved. We see a lot of the business of the Church. You feel the pressure. You get those calls. Everyone has your parents before you do. You are always sharing. Young Kids need to have impressed upon them, that they are so special, that God wanted the job of parenting them for Himself. PKs are very gifted and talented. Teenagers, as well as adults seem to be so angry. We are told to take it up with the complaint department. We do not understand what it is to have that kind of call on your life; that one may end up in the belly of whale, as Jonah. We are encouraged not to try to replace, or charge God foolishly. It is okay to be angry; but sin not. Don't let the sun go down on your wrath. That is, settle it, whatever it is, before sunset. Tell God about it. Tell Him about it. Let Him handle it. He can handle it. Be open and honest with Him. Just keep talking to Him and always trust Him.

People would stop talking when we entered the room. They would do things to my Dad that made me upset with the Church people. As a Preacher, some thought that he did not allow his people to think. Albeit, he was always concerned about the things of God.

65

There were lots of women, but a few men in Church. Everything to do with finance was in his pocket. Due to lack of respect, they grew tired of Dad organizing things. They would invite different Preachers to come in and Preach, without my Dad's knowledge. Of course, this was after he took care of all the financial woes of the Church. They finally got rid of Dad. Dad taught us to pay our tithes and give our offering. God will take care of the rest. God will take care of it. They wanted to get Dad into a desperate spot. But God helped him to prevail.

There was so much Church that we didn't have normal lives. My Parents never attended PTA meetings or school trips with us. We didn't have any friends. We could not hang out with anyone. There are four of us: three girls and one boy. Lots of pressure was put on my brother to be the golden child. I think we all need therapy because of the way we were raised. My Parents were very strict with us. Everyone looked and dressed the same. There was no individuality. He was in control of everything. The very thing he despised has consumed him. I started having problems. I felt like the world was closing in on me. I felt like I lived in a box and couldn't take it anymore. My Dad built seven Churches, but we were counted as nothing. Our names were not mentioned in his Church. Proverbs 11:30 reads: *"The fruit of the righteous is a tree of life; and he that winneth souls is wise"*. Today, when we visit his Church, we are not acknowledged. Nowadays, my Dad has other people around him.

Dad put a lot of accountability on his Children. After every service, I would hear ridicule from my Dad. Many unwise and ungodly decisions were made to protect him. There was too much criticism and not enough love shown, nor praise given to us. He would go to the homes of Church members to eat and make merry over the holidays and he still does. Mom, however, is a very sociable person. At times I thought my Dad was jealous of his wife. I feel Mom sacrificed for years being with Dad. Now, his Children and grandchildren are being sacrificed. They are hurting. I believe God is going to take care of us. It is my prayer that God will restore unto us the years that the locust, cankerworm, palmerworm and the caterpillar had eaten. God has never let me down. Give us LORD, our daily bread.

There is some anger and bitterness here at this time. It is time to forget about religion. First and foremost, it is important to have a personal one on one relationship with God. Jesus and you must work on that relationship. Have walks in the park with God. Spend some quiet time with God. Spend quality time alone with God. All of the things people are involved in will have flaws. Once you have a personal relationship with Jesus, everything else will have a different color or flavor. It is better to make a choice than to be out in a position. You never want to end up in jail, hospital and/or an accident. Make it a choice to spend time with Jesus. I encourage you to spend time with Jesus. Read the Bible for yourself. Just read it. Meditate on it for yourself. If at all possible, go to a Bible-believing Counselor that you can trust. I feel all PKs are in need of some form of counseling.

Parents in Ministry: A part of parenting is missing, especially for well-known Preachers. We were always aware of Dad and Mom missing – not being there. It is time to get some resolution so it is not looked at as an offense or crack in the armor. You must be able to put a voice to it. There is a lot of shadiness that go on in religion. We must know the difference between religion and salvation. Religion is their rush to put order in things. They are over-regulated bringing order to things, and organized disorder. Remember, everything that goes wrong in your life is because of sin. Religion is left to the interpretation of who is in charge at the movement. Rules and regulations are put into place that doesn't change as the Spirit of God moves.

"Nevertheless when it shall turn to the LORD, the vail shall be taken away. Now the LORD is that Spirit: and where the Spirit of the LORD is, there is liberty." (II Corinthians 3:16-17)

67

Joy's Story:
Granddaughter of the Bishop

My Grandmom lived with us for a while. She would get up every morning and make me breakfast before I went to school. She would take me with her to Church functions. I would sing with Grandmom at her Church services and on special programs. I love to sing and those were some very enjoyable times in my life. Everyone knew my Grandparents in my hometown. They were very loved, and respected by all who knew them. When I was in high school, if my teachers caught me acting up in class, they would say, "Do you want me to call your Grandmom Mary? The very thought of their calling my Grandmom would make me get myself together.

Years later, I went away to college. I decided while away from home that I would go to a party. Upon my arrival, this question and these statements were put before me, by another female. "What are you doing here? You shouldn't be here. You do not belong here." She did not know me. Her blunt question and statements surprised me. Needless to say, I left immediately never to return. I count it an honor and a privilege to have been born into a family of Preachers. No one called me out of my name because I am a PK. I never had any negativity shown toward me. PKs, I want you to be encouraged. You have been chosen for such a time as this. Isn't it grand?

People do not sing like they used to sing. They do not pray like they used to pray. They don't live like they used to live. One thing is certain; Jesus is coming soon. It doesn't matter who your parents are. What matters is what you have done with the gift of Jesus Christ, God's Son to the world. Can the world see Jesus in you?

"Looking unto Jesus the Author and Finisher of our faith; Who for the joy that was set before Him endured the cross, despising the shame, and is set down at the right hand of the throne of God."
(Hebrews 12:2)

Sylvia's Story

I am a Pastor's daughter, who always wanted to be treated as an individual. Some of the Church people tried to take our individuality away from us. They picked on us very often. We could never do anything right according to them. We were often accused of being the worst kind of individuals. We didn't like the label so we tried to act cooler than the coolest person. Trying to be cool did more harm to us than good. My siblings and I started smoking and using profanity. We were trying to become a part of the crowd but it was not a good idea.

When we were little, my Dad was not saved. He gambled and drank. Sometimes by the time he arrived home on payday, his paycheck was gone. There was no money to buy food or pay the bills. I thank my God today for a praying Mother. Regardless of what happened in our lives; she remained prayerful trusting in God to meet every need for her family. God always came through for us. People would come by with baskets of food for us. Mom would sit and cry, always trusting in the LORD. We never went hungry, nor lacked the necessities of life.

My Mom gave so much of herself when we were Children. At times I had feelings of neglect because people were coming so often to her for help. I wanted her to spend that time with us. Most of the people that came often were not members of our Church. They were members of the more affluent Churches in the area. Their tithes and offerings went to the Churches they attended on Sundays, but when it came to prayer they sought my Mom. They would say to her in our hearing that they could not go to their Churches because they could not get a prayer through.

Mom would tell us that God had positioned her to pray for the needs of His people. So she did. Often individuals would stay overnight in our home because of money problems. Children would also come to my Mom. She would give them lunch money if their Parents did not have any for them. We had to take less so my Parents could help the masses.

Sometimes you want Mom not the Pastor. You want that selfish Mom love but were not afforded an opportunity to experience it as a child. I now have an appreciation for the sacrifices that she gave and all of the things that she did and are doing. I vowed not to get involved as she did when I got older. Here I am today involved in Ministering to God's people and loving it. My resentment as a child has turned into an appreciation second to none. When asked now "Do you mind me calling her Mom? I say no. You are one of many Children.

I see my Mom as a dedicated Prayer Warrior for God that people can appreciate. She is an anointed woman of God with great wisdom, knowledge and understanding. She is a woman that has stood the test of time. Mom has paid her dues. For years my Mom did everything. Now as I look at all the things my Mom has done, I can only say WOW. She preserved no matter what the situation. The love of God constrained her. She has kept going down through the years. I never heard her complain and her faith never waivered. We did not think she was being realistic. Looking back now, we may have forgotten where we came from. However, we need to be careful. It is so easy to say and do the wrong thing.

Preachers' Kids, your Parent(s) did what he or she was commissioned by God to do. God has blessed them for what they have done. God's will is for you to get in a House of Worship and grow in the things of God. It is time for you to know God for yourself. If you are looking for the wrong, you will see it. He is going to ask you one day, "What did you do?" It is easy to sit and blame others. You must go to God for yourselves.

We must do what we know to be right. As PKs, we are held responsible. Whether we like it or not, it is our responsibility. We will be held accountable for what we do. Your business is how you are living for Christ. As long as you are holding onto baggage, it will not work. It is a difficult thing to see your Parent(s) go through with people. It is hard to stand by and see them hurt. Remember this, you will be paid by what you do. I will be paid for what I do.

I am not serving God for nothing. I want to be the best God wants me to be. God wants us to practice humility. I know this is easier said than done. There are some issues in our lives where we must come up. We need to stop acting holier than thou when we have not arrived yet.

I would not change the fact that my Mom is Pastor for anything in this world. It is so good to know that my Mom can get a prayer through. If I had any other Parents, I would not be the person I am today. I thank God everyday for my Mom. She is the absolute best Mom in the entire world. I praise God for her. I admire her. You know what, She is my Mentor. I realize now that I am following in her footsteps.

Spend some time in the presence of God. The answers to all of your issues can be found in the Word of God. Unblock your heart, soul, mind, body and spirit through fasting and praying. Put God in remembrance of His Word. Pray His Word back to Him. Fasting gets the wax out of your ears and puts your flesh in check. Bring your flesh under subjection to the Word and Will of God.

Tracey's Story

I am the daughter of Co-Pastors. I am not easily irritated. I refuse to let people manipulate me. My Parents taught us how to love and respect our fellow man. They gave us a lot of love and attention. My brother and I respected and loved our Parents too much to bring any shame to them. They always showed us a lot of love and concern. My brother and I were given choices. I am thankful that they did. Because we were allowed to make choices, we didn't get involved in certain things. When we would get off of the right path, sometimes it seemed that they became more loving. Our home was our sanctuary away from Church. At home, they were our Parents.

We did not have a lot of people in and out of our home. Most of the interaction my Parents had with people and Ministry while at home was via the telephone. When our home was inundated with multiple telephone calls, a twinge of jealousy would try to rear its ugly head. My brother and I would get over it rather quickly. As a Preachers' Kid, reconsider your ways. There is a lot of confusion, some of which is in the Church. Do not feed into that confusion. Your parents who were called into the Ministry need your support. Respect their position. They are anointed, appointed by God with a call on their lives. Pray for your parents. Ask God to work it out for them. Do not act out of your flesh. It is time to submit to the authority of God.

When people find out that I am a Preachers' Kid, they say, "Oh my goodness. You are a PK"? You all do everything. People do not know what to say to us. People persecuted Jesus. They put Him on the cross. It is time for you to accept the role that you are in. Our parents cannot take care of us being babies, and the babies in the church at the same time. Be encouraged to find your niche in life. When you find your niche, things will be a lot easier. Everyone was not called into the Preaching Ministry. In Bible days, the Priests were all from the Levitical Priesthood. All Priests were Levites, but all Levites were not Priest. They took care of all of the needs in the Synagogue.

Do not allow fear to overwhelm you. You need to get delivered from people. Do not allow people to control you and your ways. Act in love. Stop worrying about what people are going to say. We do not always do the right thing. Remove yourself from the appearance of nonsense. Develop our own relationship with God. Even when you make mistakes and miss it, you are still growing in God and the things of God.

To the Preacher who quit his job and is now in Ministry fulltime: you might be in error by not discussing this move with your wife and Children. Go back to your family and talk it through with them. Perchance, God has not charged you with fulltime Ministry. Your current timing may be a little off. Whatever God has called you to do, He will provide the opportunity for you. God is working it out. Keep good communication with your family. Ministry is a family mission. Talk all your decisions over with your family before making changes that will affect everyone. Pray with them. Do not let anything or anyone prevent what God has ordained for you and yours. Communication is important and timing is everything.

My brother and I were aware that we were always on display. This fact made us very aware of our surroundings. It also made us aware of what we did or said in public places. We never wanted to do, and/or say anything to bring our Parents to open shame. We love and respect them too much for that.

<u>Scriptures for Meditation</u>

"For they are life to those who find them, healing and health to all their flesh." (Proverbs 4:22 AMP)

"Consider well the path of your feet, and let all your ways be established and ordered aright." (Proverbs 4:26 AMP)

"For we are not wrestling with flesh and blood (contending only with physical opponents), but against the despotisms, against the powers, against (the master spirits who are) the world rulers of this present darkness, against the spirit forces of wickedness in the heavens, (supernatural), sphere." (Ephesians 6:12 AMP)

"For God did not give me a spirit of timidity (of cowardice, of craven and cringing and fawning fear), but (He has given us a spirit) of power and of love and of calm and well-balanced mind and discipline and self-control." (II Timothy 1:7 AMP)

"Christ purchased our freedom (redeeming us) from the curse (doom) of the law (and its condemnation) by (Himself) becoming a curse for us, for it is written (in the scriptures). Cursed is everyone who hangs on a tree (crucified)." (Galatians 3:13 AMP)

73

"For the Word that God speaks is alive and full of power (making it active, operative, energizing, and effective); it is sharper than any two-edged sword, penetrating to the dividing line of the Breath of Life (soul) and (the immortal) spirit, and of joints and marrow (of the deepest parts of our nature), exposing and sifting and analyzing and judging the very thoughts and purposes of the heart."
(Hebrews 4:12 AMP)

"Seeing then that we have a great High Priest that is passed into the heavens, Jesus the Son of God, let us hold fast our profession."
(Hebrews 4:14)

"So be subject to God. Resist the devil (stand firm against him), and he will flee from you." (James 4:7 AMP)

ACTIVATING EVENT: It is time to change your posture and position. Renew your mind with the Word of God. Stop allowing situations and circumstances to stress you out. Remember this: No problem can break you unless you let it. You have to sign for it.

BELIEF: As a man thinks in his heart, so is he. What do you believe the LORD to do for you? What do you want from the LORD? Abraham believed God and it was counted unto Him for righteousness because He called those things, which be not as though they were.

CONSEQUENCE: There are consequences to your actions. Believe you receive and you shall have it. If you truly believe, you shall receive. When will you receive it? After you believe you receive it.

If you believe an event is stressful, it will be. If you believe it is not, it won't be. It is time to take the limit off of God. Let God be God in every facet of your lives. When you focus on an activating event in your mind, it will stress you out. You become very irritated and irrational. By magnifying a situation or circumstance in your mind, you are calm and that calmness will remain.

74

Always find the good in a bad situation. See the Glass as half full, not half empty. It is time to become an optimist not a pessimist. *"And we know that all things work together for good to them that love God, to them who are the called according to His purpose."* (Romans 8:28) Most stressful events have multiple consequences. *"Casting all your care upon Him; for He careth for you."* (I Peter 5:7)

Focus on good things whenever possible. Whatever you focus on will materialize in your life. Scripture reveals that *"As a man think in his heart so is he."* (Proverbs 23:7) *"Brethren, I count not myself to have apprehended: but this one thing I do, forgetting those things which are behind, and reaching forth unto those things which are before, I press toward the mark for the prize of the high calling of God in Christ Jesus."* (Philippians 3:13-14)

Keep your inner dialogue positive. Stop the mind chatter. Control negativity. Do not allow the enemy to build a nest in your mind. *"Casting down imaginations, and every high thing that exalteth itself against the knowledge of God, and bringing into captivity every thought to the obedience of Christ;"*
(II Corinthians 10:5)

Avoid the blame game. It is natural to blame outside sources; but it escalates stress. Your pointing the finger at others for what has happened in your life is not of God. You must take responsibility for your actions. Forgive the off-ender and the offense. *"For if ye forgive men their trespasses, your heavenly Father will also forgive you: But if ye forgive not men their trespasses, neither will Your Father forgive your trespasses."*
(Matthew 6:14-15)

Many people are experiencing a great deal of stress because of pointing the finger at others. It is everyone's fault but my own. Stress will be eliminated when no one is blamed. For every action, there is a consequence. *"I, even I, am He that blotteth out thy transgressions for Mine own sake, and will not remember thy sins. Put Me in remembrance: let us plead together: declare thou, that thou mayest be justified."* (Isaiah 43:25-26)

75

Seek the face of God with your whole heart. Ask God to help you through your low and high points. When you go through the valley of the shadow of death, God is with you. Shift your focus forward to what is and can be changed by applying the Word of God. When your focus is changed, stress will be short-circuited. Line your life up with the promises of God from Genesis to Revelations. *"And be not conformed to this world: but be ye transformed by the renewing of your mind, that ye may prove what is that good, and acceptable, and perfect, will of God."*

(Romans 12:2)

Keep every situation or issue in perspective. Put all issues aside at the end of the day. Cast all your cares and concerns upon God. Do not worry about anything. Give it over to the Lord and let Him work it out. See every situation afresh in the morning. *"Remember ye not the former things, neither consider the things of old. Behold, I will do a new thing; now it shall spring forth; shall ye not know it? I will even make a way in the wilderness, and rivers in the desert."* (Isaiah 43:18-19)

Pray over whatever comes your way. Nothing is too big or too small for my God. Don't sweat the small stuff that the devil throws your way. It is all small stuff because Jesus promised never to leave you nor forsake you. The question is, *"If* God be for you, who can be against you? Therefore, *"Why art thou cast down, O my soul? and why art thou disquieted within me? hope in God for I shall yet praise Him; who is the health of my countenance, and my God".* (Psalm 43:5)

God loves you. He is concerned about every facet of your life. He doesn't want you to worry about anything. Philippians 4:8 tells us plainly what we should think on. *"Finally, brethren, whatsoever things are true, whatsoever things are honest, whatsoever things are just, whatsoever things pure, whatsoever things are lovely, whatsoever things are of good report: if there be any virtue, and if there be any praise, think on these things."* Things that are true, honest, just, pure, lovely, good reports; as well as virtue, praise, should be our focus and the center of our attention.

76

We should confidently cast all of our cares on God, knowing that He cares for us. *"So that we may boldly say, The LORD is my helper, and I will not fear what man shall do unto me."*

(Hebrews 13:6)

We must submit to God. Allow the Holy Spirit to lead and guide us into all truths. True submission to God is an act of confidence in Him. Trusting God and committing your life to His Will produces action. It is not something we put on for convenience sake. *"Submit yourselves therefore to God. Resist the devil, and he will flee from you. Draw nigh to God, and He will draw nigh to you."* (James 4:7-8a)

"IN THE BEGINNING GOD

CREATED THE HEAVEN

AND THE EARTH."

Genesis 1:1

The ISness of God

Chapter 12

"Thus saith the LORD, Let not the wise man glory in his wisdom, neither let the mighty man glory in his might, let not the rich man glory in his riches: But let him that glorieth glory in this, that he understandeth and knoweth me, that I am the LORD which exercise lovingkindness, judgment, and righteousness, in the earth: for in these things I delight, saith the LORD." (Jeremiah 9:23-24)

The ISness of God: Who is He to you? He may have healed some of you and you say, "The LORD is my healer. I tell you that He is more than that. He put a roof over your head, so you say that The LORD is my shelter, but He is more than that. You may not have had a job and He gave you gainful employment. So you say The LORD is Jehovah-Jireh, my provider. Yes, He is that and so much more. Psalm 23:1 begins with "The LORD is ...". After is, there are some dots to make it easy for you to see: The LORD is whatever you need Him to be. That is who He is. You may have been in bondage to some sickness, disease or infirmity. God came in and delivered you. So you can say: The LORD is my Deliverer; He is the Lifter of my head, except He is better than that. When we were dead in sin, lost without hope and without help, God sent Jesus to die on Calvary's cross for our sins. He redeemed us back to Himself through the shed Blood of His Son, our LORD Jesus Christ.

The LORD is Omnipresent – 'Everywhere Present' at the same time. The LORD is Omniscient – 'All Knowing'. The LORD is Omnipotent – 'All-Powerful'. The LORD is the Lifter of my head. He is my Shelter in the time of storm. He is my Food when

I am hungry. He is my Bridge over troubled waters. He is my Warhorse in the time of war. He is your Battle Axe in the time of battle. He is my Peace when I am troubled and I thank Him for that. He is everything to me, Hallelujah! I can tell you what God is for me, but you must make Him personal for you, because personal needs may differ from person-to-person. Whatever you need The LORD to be, anytime and anywhere: The LORD is to and for you. As well as, The LORD is to and for me. Hallelujah!

"Thou wilt keep him in perfect peace, whose mind is stayed on Thee: because he trusteth in Thee. Trust ye in the LORD for ever: for in the LORD JE-HO-VAH is everlasting strength:"
(Isaiah 26:3-4)

It is my desire to remind you of why we are here and where we are going. We are to show lovingkindness to mankind. The Scripture said *with lovingkindness have I drawn you.* We are to distribute to the necessity of saints through love and service. We are taught as Children to be given to hospitality or benevolence according to Romans 12:13. We care and want to serve one another as the LORD our God provides the means. Our responsibility is to serve God's people, and all humanity.

As Preachers' Kids, we must always remember the Great Commission. People are hurting. Many are in distress and pain. Countless members in the Body of Christ are in need of healing. Social Services' Ministries endeavor to meet the need of the whole man: be it spiritual, physical, emotional, social, material and/or financial. This restorative support helps to bring healing into a discernible effect.

Goals are very important. Keep your assignment ever before you. We need to focus on our charge given to us by the Almighty. Jeremiah 1:5, 8 proclaims, *"Before I formed thee in the belly I knew thee; and before thou camest forth out of the womb I sanctified thee, and I ordained thee a prophet unto the nations".* *"Be not afraid of their faces: for I am with thee to deliver thee, saith the LORD."* Examine yourselves. What are you doing? Write down your dreams and aspirations. Develop a steadfast Ministering journal. Attend workshops and seminars to assist you in meeting your mission.

Preachers' Kids constantly touch the lives of people in our Churches, communities, cities and state in accordance with Matthew 25:40. *"And the King shall answer and say unto them, Verily I say unto you, Inasmuch as ye have done it unto one of the least of these My brethren, ye have done it unto Me."* As we allow the LORD to use each of us to meet people; we are rendering benefits and services as unto the LORD. As we do good for others, we are also healing ourselves. PKs, we are family. We are units of each other. We are one.

The Bible provides wisdom, knowledge and understanding. So, what will cause Preachers' Kids, as well as family members to develop a closer relationship with God? Walking in the Spirit is vital to discipleship. Leviticus 20:7 says, *"Sanctify yourselves therefore, and be ye holy: for I AM the LORD your God"*. Prayer is talking to God. Studying God's Word is God talking to us. A good relationship with the LORD, requires us to spend time, in prayer and worship. Acting upon that can help revive every facet of our lives.

The Bible says, *"Understand this, my beloved brethren, Let every man be quick (a ready listener), slow to speak, slow to take offense and to get angry"*. (James 1:19 AMP) You have two ears and one mouth. Hint? Listen more than you speak. Think about what you want to say before you say it. Be quick to listen and slow to speak. *"He that answereth a matter before he heareth it, it is folly and shame to him."* (Proverbs 18:13) When someone is speaking and you are anticipating what they are saying and cut them off, it is wrong and dishonorable. You are not in that person's mind to predetermine what he or she might say or do. Hear the conclusion of the whole thing before you give an answer.

You might say, what is communication then? It is to impart thoughts, opinions and information through words and/or actions. It has to be successfully received, to be successfully communicated. Did you successfully communicate your message? To become a good communicator, one must first become a good listener. Others are not as interested in what we have to say as they are in what they want to say to us. Good communicators are determined by how well we listen – not how well we speak.

81

People want you to listen to them intently. Listen; just listen. Learn the art of listening and the value of using your tongue in a positive vain. Sometimes, *WE TALK TOO MUCH!* Learn to keep your mouths closed. The scripture says "And that ye s*tudy to be quiet, and to do your own business, and to work with your own hands, as we commanded you; That ye may walk honestly toward them that are without, and that ye may have lack of nothing".* (I Thessalonians 4:11-12) *"In a multitude of words there wanteth not sin: but he that refraineth his lips is wise."* (Proverbs 10:19 AMP)

We can't talk and listen at the same time. God gave us two ears and one mouth. We should be able to listen twice as much as we speak. Self-centered behavior is always demanding to speak and refusing to listen. Root cause of most conflict in interpersonal relationships is people do not listen. Take the time to listen. One complaint of Preachers' Kids is my Parents do not listen to me. They listen to other people but never take time for me. I am tired of sharing my minister parent with other people. The question on the floor is? What is the key to communications? How do you communicate? Although you are talking, are you successfully communicating?

I am the daughter of a Bishop and First Lady. My Parents taught me the difference between right and wrong. Dad set the example of a Godly man and Mom of a Godly virtuous woman of honor. My Dad was an empathetic, Christ-like man of God. He went into the community, to the homes of members and non-members alike, sharing the Good News of the Gospel, and Ministering to the need of the whole man. He was a loving and protective father. He would sit and tell us about life and the Word of God. He was a great communicator. In my hometown, he was often characterized as a 'Preacher's Pastor'.

The Bible describes a man who had an encounter with Jesus. John 5:2-9 reports the narrative this way: *"Now there is at Jerusalem by the sheep market a pool, which is called in the Hebrew tongue Bethesda, having five porches. In these lay a great multitude of impotent folk, of blind, halt, withered, waiting for the moving of the water. For an angel went down at a certain season into the pool, and troubled the water whosoever then first after the troubling of the water stepped in was made whole of whatsoever disease he had. And a certain man was there, which had an infirmity thirty and eight years. When Jesus saw him lie, and knew that he had been now a long time in that case, He saith unto him, Wilt thou be made whole? The impotent man answered Him, Sir, I have no man, when the water is troubled, to put me into the pool: but while I am coming, another steppeth down before me. Jesus saith unto him, Rise, take up thy bed, and walk. And immediately the man was made whole, and took up his bed, and walked: and on the same day was the Sabbath."*

After laying around at the pool of Bethesda for thirty-eight years; one day the impotent man met Jesus. Whenever you meet Jesus, something will happen. What is your experience? Your Dad and Mom may have broken up. Nowadays, your Dad will not help you. You talk to the Pastor and say, "You do not know my situation." The question on the floor is: Do you want to get up? If you do, Jesus will help you get up. It doesn't matter how things look, or the circumstances; do you want to get up? Do you really want to get up? God is raising us up. "Then said He unto His disciples, The harvest truly is plenteous, but the laborers are few; Pray ye therefore the Lord of the harvest, that He will send forth laborers into His harvest." (Matthew 9:37-38)

You must decide that you will not be last any more. Do you want to get up? No more excuses. No more talking. Let us get up and do something. Schools are closing while people are opening prisons all over the country. The prisons today are all state-of-the-art. Many schools have the same equipment for decades. The rich are likely to get richer, while the poor gets poorer. God has blessed us with life. I Timothy 6:6-8 encourages: *"But godliness with contentment is great gain. For we brought nothing into this world, and it is certain we can carry nothing out. And having food and raiment let us be therewith content."* Many people have a heart for Public Service: Be it urban, city, state, suburban and/or country. Do you desire to change? Wake up. You can implement change. Don't forget where you came from, or where you are going. Do you want to change? You need to do something affirmative for yourself. You are more dynamic than material possessions.

Man, how are you treating your wife? Woman, how are you treating your husband? How are both of you treating your Children? Single persons, how are you treating yourselves? How are we all treating our parents? Exodus 20:12 says, *"Honor thy father and thy mother: that thy days may be long upon the land which the LORD thy God giveth thee."* By the Grace of God, we (you) have the ability to rise up above any situation. The man by the pool of Bethesda had been in the same condition for years. Finally, Jesus came by. He told Jesus all about his past. He could not fathom change. Jesus was there to change his deep-seated lingering disorder. When the man tried to get into the water, no one would help him. All he saw was dysfunction. You can't put your faith in man. Man will fail you. Can't anybody do you like Jesus? Once your perception accepts impairment as normal from your reality, then dysfunction becomes ordinary. However, it seems crazy, when dysfunction becomes normal and perception becomes your reality. Some come to see it as normal. No matter the situation, Jesus is always there for you.

Fruit of the Spirit

"But the fruit of the (Holy) Spirit (the work which His presence accomplishes) is love, joy (gladness), peace, patience (an even temper, forbearance), kindness, goodness (benevolence), faithfulness, Gentleness (meekness, humility), self-control (self-restraint, continence). Against such things there is no law (that can bring a charge)." (Galatians 5:22-23 AMP)

Love is the hammer. Joy is the electricity. When you need a jolt, plug into it. Peace is the walls. Longsuffering is the foundation. Gentleness is the insulation. Meekness is the nails. Temperance is the plumbing. Faith is the bricks, purifying. The wise pig built his house out of bricks. The contractor is Jesus Christ. His natural dad was a carpenter named Joseph. Jesus wants to build your house and work out your situation. Let Him work it out, in you and for you. God has given you a vision. He will bring it to pass. *"Let us hold fast the profession of our faith without wavering; (for He is faithful that promised);"* (Hebrews 10:23)

84

Chapter 13

I have called you for a Divine purpose to show My people, My love. You have been call to rebuild the old waste places; to root up, to tear down pre-conceived ideas about the LORD. The LORD has set before you an open door that no one can shut according to Revelation 3:8. Do not listen to the negativity around you. I am leading and guiding you in every situation. You are Mine. I love you. When you come into a situation, things change. You bring My presence. They act funny because they do not follow Me. Yes, some say they do but there is no personal relationship.

"Ye have not chosen Me, but I have chosen you, and ordained you, that ye should go and bring forth fruit, and that your fruit should remain: that whatsoever ye shall ask of the Father in My name, He may give it you." (John 15:16) My son, daughter, I have chosen you. I love you. I want you to know that you were made in My image and likeness. I want what is best for you. You are an example of what I can and will do in the lives of someone who takes Me at My Word. Yield yourself to Me. I have brought you here for a reason and a purpose. You are on My assignment.

"Being confident of this very thing, that He which hath begun a good work in you will perform it until the day of Jesus Christ:" (Philippians 1:6) Open your mouth; I will speak for you. Don't be apprehensive about anything. I am in control of your life and your circumstances. You have been faithful over a few things. I will make you a ruler over many things. You are Mine. No one can pluck you out of My hands.

"The blessing of the LORD, it maketh rich, and He [God] addeth no sorrow with it." (Proverbs 10:22) I am supplying all your need; giving you the desires of your heart, blessing you above measure; making you the head and not the tail; a lender and not a borrower; above only; you shall never be beneath. I have blessed you above measure. Your name demands favor; your silhouette demands favor; your voice demands favor and your person demands favor. No one can curse you. As Balaam tried to curse the Children of Israel and He could only bless them. Anyone that tries to curse you, can only bless you, because you are blessed and highly favored of the LORD.

Abraham's blessings are (ours) yours. God has overturned everything, every scheme of the enemy. Total restoration in all things is yours. Let go of the past. This is a new day. *"Remember ye not the former things, neither consider the things of old. Behold, I will do a new thing; now it shall spring forth; shall ye not know it? I will even make a way in the wilderness, and rivers in the desert."* (Isaiah 43:18-19) You are the apple of God's eye. He has promised never to leave you (us) nor forsake you (us). God has prepared a table before you (us) in the presence of your (our) enemies. *"Thou preparest a table before me in the presence of mine enemies: thou anointest my head with oil; my cup runneth over."* (Psalm 23:5) Every hindrance has been removed. *"But as it is written, EYE HAS NOT SEEN, NOR EAR HEARD, NEITHER HAVE ENTERED INTO THE HEART OF MAN, THE THINGS WHICH GOD HATH PREPARED FOR THEM THAT LOVE HIM."* (I Corinthians 2:9)

Just relax in the LORD. Trust Him. Don't lean on your own understanding. *Acknowledge the LORD in all your ways and He will direct your path.* Stop worrying. *Cast all your cares upon the LORD for He cares for you. Delight yourself in the LORD. He will give you the desire of your heart.* Remember, this is your season, your year of jubilee.

Father, open the eyes of my understanding so that I may know who I am in You. Teach me how to walk the way Jesus walked. Thank You for leading me by the Holy Spirit. Thank You for the power to do what You would have me to do.

86

"So shall My Word be that goeth forth out of My mouth: it shall not return unto Me void, but it shall accomplish that which I please, and it shall prosper in the thing whereto I sent it." (Isaiah 55:11)

"There shall no evil befall thee, neither shall any plague come nigh thy dwelling. For He shall give His angels charge over thee, to keep thee in all thy ways." (Psalm 91:10-11)

"The angel of the LORD encampeth round about them that fear Him, and delivereth them." (Psalm 34:7)

"He personally bore our sins in His (own) body on the tree (as on an altar and offered Himself on it), that we might die (cease to exist) to sin and live to righteousness. By His wounds you have been healed," (I Peter 2:24 AMP)

"And thus He fulfilled what was spoken by the prophet Isaiah. He Himself took (in order to carry away) our weaknesses and infirmities and bore away our diseases," (Matthew 8:17 AMP)

"Surely He has borne our griefs (sicknesses, weaknesses, and diseases) and carried our sorrows and pains (of punishment), Yet we (ignorantly) considered Him stricken, smitten and afflicted by God (as if with leprosy. But HE was wounded for our transgressions, He was bruised for our guilt and iniquities, the chastisement (needful to obtain) peace and well being for us was upon Him, and with the stripes (that wounded) Him we are healed and made whole," (Isaiah 53:4-5 AMP)

"For the law of the Spirit of Life (which is) in Christ Jesus (the law of our new being) has freed me from the law of sin and of death,"
(Romans 8:2 AMP)

"For the weapon of our warfare are not physical (weapons of flesh and blood) but they are mighty before God for the overthrow and destruction of strongholds," (II Corinthians 10:4 AMP)

"Put on God's whole armor (the armor of a heavy-armed soldier which God supplies), that you may be able successfully to stand up against (all) the strategies and the deceits of the devil, Lift up over all the (covering) shield of saving faith, upon which you can quench all the flaming missiles of the wicked (one)," (Ephesians 6:11, 16 AMP)

"He who dwells in the secret place of the Most High shall remain stable and fixed under the shadow of the Almighty (whose power no foe can withstand)," (Psalm 91:1 AMP)

"He shall not be afraid of evil things, his heart is firmly fixed, trusting (leaving on and being confident) in the Lord,"
(Psalm 112:7 AMP)

"Saying, If you will diligently hearken to the voice of the LORD your God and will do what is right in His sight, and will listen to and obey His commandments and keep all His statues, I will put none of the diseases upon you which I brought upon the Egyptians, for I am the LORD who heals," (Exodus 15:26 AMP)

"See now that I, even I, am He, and there is no god with Me: I kill, and I make alive; I wound, and I heal: neither is there any that can deliver out of My hand." (Deuteronomy 32:39)

People have many unrealistic expectations of Preachers' Kids. We must be above reproach. They see us as miniature images of God because our Parent(s) are Ministers. There is always so much pressure to be perfect in the eyes of everyone who is aware of our status. Sometimes it seems that a sign is attached to you saying: "I should be perfect because I am a Preachers' Kid. Examine me. Put me under a microscope. See if I can measure up to what you expect a Preacher's Kid to do and be". You are a marked person who is expected to be better than most people If you are perceived as such, then you will be labeled as a snob or high echelon person. How can I ever measure up to what's expected of me? Can I be my own person with my own personality, or shall I try to imitate my Parents?

What if I were not born a Preachers' Kids? I wish I didn't have to be something I can't live up to. How can I live up to your expectation of me? I am not perfect. It seems I am making more mistakes while trying to live up to your expectations. The pressure of being perfect is sometimes over whelming. It causes me to do things I would not have done if I were not looking for the approval of man.

We are always held to a higher standard. This ought not be. Being judged by others should be taboo. We wish we didn't always have to be on display, because of who our Parents are. There is a stigma attached to Children of The Reverend Clergy. The status quo is this: You are held accountable because you are hanging out with the Preacher. They expect all Preachers' Kids to be like a little Jesus. We should behave the way Jesus probably behaved when He walked upon the earth.

Preachers' Kids, you may see people experimenting with various things, but you stay clear. You are held to a higher standard. Even sinners expect your life to be above reproach. While in college, one of my nieces attended a party on campus. When she arrived at the party, someone said to her. "What are you doing here? You know you do not belong here." She said she looked at her clothes and wondered if she was wearing a sign saying PK. Remember this, you are judged by the company you keep, the things you say, the clothes you wear and the things that you do. You are judged because you live in the same home with the Preacher. It is often said of you that if you can't get it right in the Preachers' home, how can anyone expect their Children to live the abundant life in Christ?

Minister Parents must let their Children know who they are and what is expected of them. They must encourage their Children to hold their heads up high. My Dad told us "Never let anyone put you down because of the color of your skin, what you have or do not have. You are as good as or better than anyone walking on two feet." Growing up in the segregated South, many challengers faced us. But the fact that my Dad was the Bishop and both Parents were

Radio personalities, helped my siblings and me. We were not exposed to a lot of the racism because of our Minister Parents. Today, our Parents are still highly respected throughout the surrounding communities in South Carolina. Thank God. When any of us go home, we often hear people whispering, "that's Bishop and Mother Bowens' Children and/or grandchildren".

"LORD, Thou hast been our dwelling place in all generations. Before the mountains were brought forth, or ever thou hadst formed the earth and the world, even from everlasting to everlasting, Thou art God." (Psalm 90:1-2)

Just be the individual God made you. Don't try to measure up to the expectations of others. Know God is the keeper and not you yourself. Remember Job? His perfection was not found in what he did but who he was. Do not live by the expectations of others but be all God wants you to be. Know God is watching and waiting for you. David made mistakes written in history but he had a heart that turned back to God. God called David, "A man after His own heart." David was quick to forgive and swift to repent for wrong doings. Don't allow past offenses to keep you away from God. He is waiting for you (for us) to repent and return to Him.

Chapter 14

God has called you into the Ministry of soul winning. He who wins souls is wise. In your zest to please God, you sometimes run ahead of Him. You may not always take time to adequately seek the face of God. Matthew 6:33, tells us to, *"Seek first the Kingdom of God and His righteousness"*. Did you seek the face of God? Are you studying to show yourself approved unto God? Are you rightly dividing, the Word of truth according to the Bible? *"Study to shew thyself approved unto God, a workman that needeth not to be ashamed, rightly dividing the Word of truth."* (II Timothy 2:15)

Someone told you or coerced you in believing that the Ministry comes first and you believed them. Why? *"You did run well; who did hinder you that you should not obey the truth,"* (Galatians 5:7) Everyone and everything else is second. So, what did you do? Well, you quit your job without discussing it with your family. You said that it was done for the sake of the Ministry. Yet your family is suffering because of it. You insist that you had an epiphany in regard to leaving your job.

Did God make clear to you to suspend secular work? Otherwise, did people persuade you to quit? *YOU MAY HAVE THOUGHT YOU COULD WALK BEFORE YOU COULD CRAWL, SO YOU QUIT YOUR JOB.* Nevertheless, if you do quit your job, in spite of everything, always know that what God requires, He provides the enablement. Psalm 46:10 advises, *"Be still, and know that I am God: I will be exalted among the heathen, I will be exalted in the earth"*. Having a discussion with your family, regarding the

91

possibility of quitting, may bring more light to the conversation. Always look at the big picture. Consider all persons concerned, whose lives may be affected by any decision. Our God IS*!!* As an old song runs: "God is a Right Now God, YES HE IS*!* He May not Come When You Want Him, But He is Always Right on Time. He is a Right Now God, YES HE IS"*!* May you and your family continue to be blessed. *"The LORD shall increase you more and more, you and your Children. Ye are blessed of the LORD which made heaven and earth."* (Psalm 115:14-15)

Your attitude says *GOD has called me and I do not have to discuss my decision with any man. I AM a man. I AM a woman. GOD has called me and I will not let anyone stand in my way.* Here you are telling your family with everyone else from the pulpit about your decision to quit your job. The LORD told me to quit my job and go into full time Christian service. I quit work on Friday. I gave them my notice. Friday was my last day. It doesn't matter to me what anyone thinks, I am being obedient to God and His call on my life. In the meantime, you are not providing for your family. They do not have the basic necessities. They are now suffering in silence. You feel justified as you go from place to place in your three-piece suit. Your family is suffering needlessly. You are causing them to resent God and the things of God by your actions.

When your Spouse comes to you to clear the air, you will not give her an ear to listen. You need to get rid of your selfish acts. Let go and let God. Go to your wife and Children. Ask them to forgive you. Pray that God will heal your relationship with the members of your immediate family. Tell your wife how much you love her and need her help in the Ministry. This is not your Ministry alone. Tell your wife and Children, it is our Ministry. We are in this together. I need you with me. I need your help. I can't do this alone. I need you or this will not work. You are important to me. The only person in front of your wife is God. You must honor your parents, respect your wife, take care of your Children, and love God with all your heart and your neighbor as yourself.

Stop making your wife and Children feel like an after-thought. Let them know continually how important they are to you.

92

Include them in decision-making that will affect their lives; "Lest Satan should get an advantage of us: for we are not ignorant of his devices" (II Corinthians 2:11) Jesus cautions about three devices in John 10:10. *"The thief cometh not, but for to steal, and to kill, and to destroy: I am come that they might have life and that they might have it more abundantly"*. Jesus came that we might have and enjoy life to the fullest until it overflows. Get your family involved in decisions and listen to their input. When you take heed to what they have to say; most opposition will be removed. Your spouse is your Helpmate. 'Let her help you.' You will receive favor from the LORD because of your wife. *"Whoso findeth a wife findeth a good thing, and obtaineth favour of the LORD,"* (Proverbs 18:22) You have given your attention beyond them. It is never too late to recant, nor change what has occurred. You can reach out to your spouse, and children now. Ask them to forgive you. Allow me to reiterate again: While many of you are Ministering to the world, countless numbers of your families are being forsaken.

Cultivate a relationship with them individually and collectively. It is never too late to show love to your spouse and children. Forgive yourself for not being there for them. Ask God to forgive you. Move forward. Be encouraged to hug them and spend quality time with them. Your Children will reciprocate when you reach out to them.

Spouse

Tell your Spouse, God said in Genesis, chapter 2:24, *"Therefore shall a man leave his father and his mother, and shall cleave unto his wife: and they shall be one flesh."* However, you have behaved as though the two of you are separate. How can you repay her for your error? You can't compensate her by words only. You can only give back through deeds and actions. There is no payback. Genuine change can only be had, due to love and kindness. If you are willing to correct and fix what may have been broken over the years; God promises restoration.

He wants you to know that there is a Word for you in Joel 2:25. *"And I will restore to you the years that the locust hath eaten, the cankerworm, and the caterpillar, and the palmerworm, my great army which I sent among you. And ye shall eat in plenty, and be satisfied, and praise the name of the LORD your God, that hath dealt wondrously with you: and my people shall never be ashamed."* Demonstrate love and devotion to your family. It is a family Ministry. Go to your family before going to God and ask them for forgiveness. Conversely, without God, it will not work.

The Offspring of The Reverend Clergy is in need of a total healing. This healing should include spiritual, mental, physical, social, financial, emotional and material. The hurts experienced are so deeply rooted and surrounded in fear. The enemy of your soul is trying to destroy you. It is time for you to face your hurts. Deal with self. Do you know who you are? It is time for you to *know* who you are. Take off the mask. First, *"to thine own self be true"*. If you are not transparent with you, I know you will not be with anyone else.

The pain festering in your mind, body, spirit and life is not from God. The pain has brought fear. The fear brought you torment. Let us deal with the fear first. Psalm 23:4 says, *"I will fear no evil for Thou art with me."* I will fear no evil. Who is the Thou with you? Do you know who He is? He is Jehovah God, ELELYON. The Most High God is with you. I will fear no evil for Jesus is with me. I will fear no evil for the Holy Ghost is with me. I will fear no evil for Goodness and Mercy is following me. Jesus said, He will never leave me nor forsake me. He will be with me until the end. Therefore, I will fear no evil. Psalm 27:1 *says "The Lord is my light and my salvation; whom shall I fear? The Lord is the strength of my life; of whom shall I be afraid?" "For God hath not given us the spirit of fear; but of power, and of love, and of a sound mind,"* (II Timothy 1:7)

Fear has torment. *"Cast down imaginations and every high thing that would exalt itself against the knowledge of God and bringing into captivity every thought to the obedience of Christ,"* (II Corinthians 10:5) Receive your healing today. Luke 9:11 shows

94

kindness. *"And the people, when they knew it, followed Him: and He received them, and spake unto them of the kingdom of God, and healed them that had need of healing."* This is not just a physical healing. This is a total healing. Shalom – wholeness, nothing missing, nothing broken. Brokenness, lack, sickness, disease, infirmity, poverty all come from the enemy of your soul. Wellness, wholeness, healing, prosperity and all good things come from God.

To the Offspring of The Reverend Clergy, let go and let God have His way in your lives. "But s*eek ye first the kingdom of God, and His righteousness; and all these things shall be added unto you."* (Matthew 6:33) Seek God's face, not His hands, with all your heart. Stop penalizing us because God called our Parent(s) into the Ministry. We are not perfect people, neither are our Parents. We shed tears, feel joy, pain, sorrow, excitement and experience other emotions. The same sentiments that you feel, we feel. When we stand before the Bema Seat – Judgment Seat of Christ, we will all be judged the same. We are not perfect but we (mankind – those who accept Christ) are striving toward perfection.

Preacher: Stop trying to make your Children into angelic beings and not flesh and blood Children. They will become angry, resentful and rebellious toward God, the Ministry and you. Do not allow outsiders to cause your Children unnecessary pain and discomfort. This will push them from God to serve satan, who will use Church folk to provoke them to sin.

Your Children can be so damaged because you are so prideful or thinking you have arrived is not of God. You shall be judged for this behavior. Treating your Children with disdain and contempt because of what people are saying about their attitudes and actions are wrong. Why are you putting so much pressure on them? As a Minister, as quiet as it is kept, you are not perfect. All perfect people are home with the LORD. As my Dad once Preached, *"What Are You Doing When No One Is Looking"*? We are all red blooded individuals born into a Preacher's family. Some of us had stricter rules and regulations than others

Parents, accept us as we are and encourage your Congregations to do the same. My Dad and Mom had family meetings with us weekly to air our concerns. Daily, we were encouraged to be ourselves. We were not perfect but we were loved, encouraged and disciplined by Parents who were sold out to God but they were not perfect people either. No one is perfect in their own strength. As long as we live in this flesh, it is an enemy of God.

Dad and Mom did not spare the Word of God or the rod of correction. We were praised when we did well and were chastised when we didn't. They taught us God's Word at home and Church. We had family prayer and family share time. We were not pushed into a Preaching Ministry, but we were always encouraged to love God with all our hearts and live exclusively for Him accepting Jesus as our LORD. When negative things were said by outsiders; Dad would nip it in the bud by explaining to us never to let anyone put you down for any reason because of what you do or do not have. You are as good as or better than anyone walking on two feet. *Let every man be a liar, but let God be true.* God's Word will stand forever. Dad loved us and we knew it. My sisters and I were 'his Gals' and my brothers 'his sons'. He loved us and taught us to be the best we could be. He is at home with the LORD now, but we still speak very warmheartedly of his love, and care for Mom and their Children. May God bless their memory.

As I write this book, my Mom is ninety years old. She is a virtuous woman of honor. She loves us and prays for us in season and out of season. Our precious Lady, an honorable woman of good reputation is the *love of our lives.* Dad always let Mom be her own person. She loves the LORD with all her heart. We were always encouraged to show love and kindness everywhere we went. *"Mom, I want to be like you when I grow up."* Our Parents lived honorable and Holy lives before us. We can go out into the world and show others the love of God because of Dad and Mom. They did not beat us over the head with the Bible. I thank God that they dealt with each of us at our own level of understanding. As a result, my siblings and I do not resent God, the Church or our Parents. We know God experientially, through Godly teaching and Holy living of our Parents, in out of our home. This is what made the difference

96

in our lives. The opinions voiced by outsiders were not allowed to hurt us. It was like water on a duck's back.

Dad was his own person; a man after God's own heart. Mom was a strong woman and his beloved wife. We were his Children; their Children. Dad and Mom, together, made our house a home. Our environment was filled with love; a place where our family, as well as so many others sought refuge. The love of God was shared with us and with those they came in contact with.

The breakdown is as follows: Dad, Mom and a family of eleven Children. (May God bless the memory of those who are no longer with us). The three oldest children died in early childhood. Eight of us grew up together: three brothers and five sisters. One sister, a Missionary and singer left us in August 1997. Her former husband is a Deacon, a General Educational Development (GED) instructor and a retired law enforcement officer. Their children are still dealing with the lost of their young Mom. Their daughter is a brilliant photographer. One brother, a dynamic charismatic Preacher went home to be with the LORD in November 1998. He worked for a large Telecom company assisting the deaf. He was also the Social Services' Director at a large Church. His former wife is a Phlebotomist. One of their sons, an engineer, is a Pastor/Missionary. Their other son is an entrepreneur.

Today, there are six of us: One brother is a Bishop/Pastor and a retired Military Veteran. His wife is a nurse. Their Children are super-talented. One daughter is a stationery and print designer. One brother, a retired Metro bus driver, is an ordained Minister and a musician. His wife is retired law enforcement. Their Children are smart and talented. One daughter is in the Military Reserves. One sister is a Missionary and an exceptional singer. Her late husband was awarded a Purple Heart during the Vietnam War. Their Children are highly accomplished. One daughter, upon graduating college, was inducted into the National Honor Society. One sister, an amazing singer, is a healthcare professional, BSN. Her husband, a Vietnam-era Veteran, is a retired law enforcement officer. Their Children are all over-achievers. One of their daughters is a Military Physician. One sister, an education advocate, has a Law degree. Her late husband was an ordained Minister. He volunteered as a Cleric to hospitals and those in need. Their Children are highly motivated to succeed. One son is a successful Restaurateur. One sister is me: The Reverend Doctor Arnetha Bowens. I am the Author of this book, "Preachers' Kids: Living In Glass Houses".

We are certainly blessed and honored to be PKs. The next generation are artists, authors, Clerics, doctors, engineers, entrepreneurs, law enforcement, mechanics, merchandisers, musicians, scholars, teachers, etc. We are occupied in prayer, study, and employment. We hope to do our part, in making this world a better place. While growing up in the South, our Parents worked tireless to make something of all of us. They loved us so much. We are so appreciative and indebted to their memory. Most of all, we are thankful to God for choosing righteous parents for us. We could not have asked for better. There is no one better than they were. Praise the LORD. God has done great things, for us and through us.

They loved us, provided for us, sacrificed for us and trained us in the way we should go. God's Word is true. Now that we are older, we have not departed from their teaching. Although we are all adults, we are still in love with God and His Word, "that is a lamp unto our feet and a light unto our paths". We are not perfect, but Jesus is sitting on the throne of our heart houses. We are growing daily in the things of the LORD. We are expecting God to order our steps on a daily basis. The Great Commission was given to everyone. God has called all of us (*mankind)* to go into the world and Preach (*be witnesses*) the Gospel to every creature *(on earth)*.

We often reminisce about our childhood and thank God for our training. Dad and Mom were Radio personalities for more than forty years. A few years ago, due to stress, Mom had a brain attack also known as a *stroke*. Since that time, I have taken some tiny steps in their shoes. I am presently carrying on their legacy on WJAY 1280 AM Radio in South Carolina, to the Glory and Honor of God our Father. What an honor and a privilege to be chosen by God, for such a time as this, to Preach the Good News of the Gospel of Jesus Christ. To God Be the Glory for All He has done.

Preachers' Kids

Who Are These People?

Chapter 15

These people, Preachers' Kids, feel like they are a forgotten group. Their Parents are out, evangelizing the world, while many of them have gone astray. Many have lost sight of God and the things of God. They are feeling ostracized, rejected, detested, unloved and unwanted. There is a battle going on in their minds to do evil and not good. The Fact: Parents are busy saving the world; while not taking an active interest in the needs of their Children. Fact: Ministry activities and events create a perception of disregard and neglect. This can cause resentment of God, the Church, the Synagogue, the Temple, as well as the Things of God.

A portion of this group has turned to lives of crime, drugs, dropped out of society and some have even committed suicide. Yes, suicide. Many individuals in this group are practicing their Parents' faith mechanically. Yet, some are actually living the life they sing and talk about – devotion to the Only True and Living God, Jehovah Jirah, ADONAI, YHWH, ELELYON – The Most High God. We need to encourage and strengthen the Children of The Reverend Clergy, letting them know first and foremost that they are not alone. Help them to get in touch with their feelings – be it love, anger, resentment, jealousy, envy, strife, joy, peace, goodness and gladness. We all need to be motivated to do and to be all we can. When we realize that the sky is the limit: our trust in God is able to grow, from "faith to faith". This group needs to be encouraged to turn back to God. He did not let them down. God loves each and every one of them. *"Casting all your care upon Him; for He careth for you."* (I Peter 5:7)

Teach them to look for the good in what seems to be a bad situation. Help them to see the glass half full rather than half empty. Focus on the good or positive things in life. According to sacred scripture, *"Finally, brethren, whatsoever things are true, whatsoever things are honest, whatsoever things are just, whatsoever things are pure, whatsoever things are lovely, whatsoever things are of good report; if there be any virtue, and if there be any praise, think on these things".* (Philippians 4:8) Avoid the blame game. It escalates stress. Keep inner dialogue positive. Always maintain a positive mental attitude.

"Yea, they may forget, yet will I not forget thee. Behold, (see) I have graven thee upon the palms of My hands; thy walls are continually before me." (Isaiah 49:15b-16 AMP)

Offspring of The Reverend Clergy, God has us always on His mind. Many are in dire need of a total healing. This healing should include, but not be limited to spiritual, mental, physical, social, financial, emotional and material needs. The hurts and suffering can be so deeply rooted. Pain can become surrounded with anxiety and fear. Fear has torment. *"For God hath not given us the spirit of fear; but of power, and of love, and of a sound mind."* (II Timothy 1:7)

Face YOUR Hurts

The enemy of your soul is trying to destroy you. It is time to face all of those hurts. Deal with your self. Get to know who you are *and most of all whose you are.* By all means, take off the mask. First, to "thine own self be true". The pain festering in your mind, body, spirit and life is not of God. The pain you are experiencing has brought you fear. The fear has brought you torment. It is time to let go and let God have His way in you. Are you up for the challenge?

Let's deal with your fears first. Psalm 23:4 says *I will fear no evil for Thou art with me.* I will fear no evil. Who is the Thou with you? Jehovah God is with you. I will fear no evil for Jesus is

100

with you. I will fear no evil for The Holy Ghost is with me. I will fear no evil for the twins; Goodness and Mercy are following me all the days of my life. Jesus said, *"He would never leave us nor forsake us"*. (See Hebrews 13:5-6) He will be with us until the end.

I will fear no evil. *"The LORD is my light and my salvation; whom shall I fear? the LORD is the strength of my life; of whom shall I be afraid?"* (Psalm 27:1) *"For God hath not given us the spirit of fear; but of power, and of love, and of a sound mind."* (II Timothy 1:7) *"There is no fear in love; but perfect love casteth out fear: because fear hath torment. He that feareth is not made perfect in love."* (I John 4:18) There is nothing but torment in fear. Unconditional love is essential to peace.

It isn't possible to express the importance of this way of thinking enough. *"Casting down imaginations, and every high thing that exalteth itself against the knowledge of God, and bringing into captivity every thought to the obedience of Christ;"* (II Corinthians 10:5) Receive your healing today. [Jesus] *"Healed them that had need of healing"*. (Luke 9:11) Jesus always had compassion on those that followed Him. He healed them. He encouraged them. He fed them. He cared about the needs of the people. How do you care for others?

I speak Shalom: completeness, wholeness (nothing missing, nothing broken) over you life. The brokenness, lack, sickness, disease, infirmity and poverty have come from the enemy of your soul. Abundance, healing, wellness wholeness, as well as wealth and prosperity come from God. Know that the LORD is your (our) Shepherd and you (we) shall not want.

Offspring of The Reverend Clergy: Let go and let God. Seek God. *"But seek ye first the kingdom of God, and His righteousness; and all these things shall be added unto you,"* (Matthew 6:33) Seek His face with all your heart. I encourage you to read and commit to memory Psalm 27 in its entirety. Make it your own. Spiritually insert your name in there and your family member's, as well as other loved ones.

The Vision

"I will stand upon my watch, and set me upon the tower, and will watch to see what He will say unto me, and what I shall answer
when I am reproved. And the LORD answered me, and said, write the vision, and make it plain upon tables, that he may run that readeth it. For the vision is yet for an appointed time, but at the end it shall speak, and not lie: though it tarry, wait for it; because it will surely come, it will not tarry. Behold, his soul which is lifted up is not upright in him: but the Just shall live by his faith."

(Habakkuk 2:2-4)

We should rehearse God's history. It re-affirms our faith. While it is time consuming, spend time with God. Spend time with God in the midst of your pain and suffering, Forget the impossibilities. Let God's Word resonate in your heart. You might say, "God, it looks impossible", but so did the Red Sea. God, it looks so impossible, but so did the Walls of Jericho. LORD, it looks unattainable, but so did occupying the Promised Land. God has done so many great and mighty things for us. If you would check from Genesis through Revelations, the half has not been told. Spend time seeking God's face. Let Him put His purpose into your heart.

God sent the east wind and backed up the Red Sea – more than 6 million Jews walked across on dry ground. It was not a feeble one among them. Not one of them got a splash on them. If God could do that then, He can do that now. When you are struggling with situations/circumstances wondering how God is coming through for you, the first thing to do is to look back at His history. Can your God do what He said? Is He able to do what He promised? If He promised to do something and you did not like it, can you trust His integrity?

It doesn't matter what your situation may be, we should give thanks to God. II Thessalonians 5:18 says, *"In everything give thanks for this is the will of God in Christ Jesus concerning you"*. When you open your mouth and begin to lift up the name of Jesus, you will begin to understand why He sent the rain and the storm.

102

Why He held back the blessing? While you were locked in prison, give God praise. Rehearse God's History in praise.

You must believe God. You must take Him at His Word. Did God ever do anything for you? Has He given you your hearts desire at any time? Are your needs met? I encourage you to go back to the beginning. When you stand up, you should have some history to talk about. Think about what He did for you in your Genesis. He made you in His own image and likeness; then blew breath into your body and you became a living soul. Hallelujah!

Exodus: He brought you out by His Outstretched Arm, Strong Power and Mighty Arm, with riches and great wealth in excellent health. Think about your history. Think on how He brought your family out. Pause and reflect on all God has done for you and give Him praise.

"THE EYES OF YOUR UNDERSTANDING
BEING ENLIGHTENED; THAT YE MAY
KNOW WHAT IS THE HOPE OF HIS
CALLING, AND WHAT THE RICHES OF
THE GLORY OF HIS INHERITANCE
IN THE SAINTS."

Ephesians 1:18

Chapter 16

God has no limits or boundaries. Satan has limitations. He is a created being. I encourage you to get to know the Creator. When satan bothers you, seek the face of God. Continue seeking God until He intervenes. Satan cannot read your mind. Recognize negative thoughts and cast them down. The Bible says: *"resist the devil and he will flee from you"*. Know who you are in God.

Gullible Christians believe almost anything. They tend to believe every preacher they hear. These precious saints are easy to fleece, because they are so trusting. They look everywhere for services to attend. They possess Bibles, yet they are always in search of a Word from the LORD. Words are spoken to them such as: "God told me to tell you". *These can be dangerous words.* Satan comes as an angel of light. God can speak to us through signs and wonders. He may speak through dreams, visions and even quietness. Nonetheless, it is wise to rely fully on God's Word, The Holy Bible.

"And He [God] said, Go forth, and stand upon the mount before the LORD. And, before, the LORD passed by, and a great and strong wind rent the mountains, and brake in pieces the rocks before the LORD; but the LORD was not in the wind: and after the wind an earthquake; but the LORD was not in the earthquake. And after the earthquake a fire; but the LORD was not in the fire: and after the fire a still small voice." (I Kings 19:11-12)

"For thus saith the Lord God, the Holy One of Israel; In returning and rest shall ye be saved; in quietness and in confidence shall be your strength:" (Isaiah 30:5a)

Know them that labor among you. Get to understand the character of those who are in your inner and outer circle. Know your faith in Christ. You must have faith in God. Know in whom you believe. Be persuaded that He is able to keep that which you have committed into His hands against that day.

You are the righteousness of God in Christ Jesus. Do you know who you are? God's Word, the Bible will stand the test of time. Resist the devil and fight back. You are not wrestling against flesh and blood according to Ephesians 6:12 *"For we wrestle not against flesh and blood, but against principalities, against powers, against the rulers of the darkness of this world, against spiritual wickedness in high places."*

Reality Check

Preachers' Kids, "You are on display". Someone is always listening and watching everything we say and do. It doesn't matter where we go or what we do, someone is watching. You are constantly on display as you go about your day-to-day activities. I want you to always remember this: *You live in a Glass House.* You might say why? Why must I live in a Glass House? Why am I on public display? My life is not an open book. My parents' lives are but not mine. I want my privacy.

Allow me to explain something to you. The world sees our Minister Parent(s) as being next to God. They are God's mouthpieces. They are being compared to God and the things of God. They are His representatives here on this earth. Perfection and greatness are expected from them and their posterity. Did you not know that, *"You Live in A Glass House"?* Your life is always under close scrutiny in and out of Church, school, the community and the family. Some people feel your Minister Parent(s) are (should be) perfect. You might ask why? Well, they do spend a lot of time in God's presence seeking guidance and direction? They are studying His Word, right? I remember in the Bible when people spent time with God their lives changed. They didn't tolerate sin and/or foolishness.

"We Are Living in Glass Houses." We are always on display. More is expected of us because we live under the same roof as the Minister. We shouldn't desire to engage in anything but something Biblical. If it is not scriptural-based, we should avoid it at any cost is the attitude of the Parents of the non-Preacher Kids. It is scandalous for us to desire participation in sports, drama, and/or anything not biblically based. We should know better than to try is often the common misconception.

Everything we do and say is compared to spiritual things. The fact that we are the Offspring of The Reverend Clergy sets us apart as super spiritual. We automatically have little halos on. Big brother and/or sister are always watching to see if our halos are crooked or not. We are held as a model for their Children. The Scripture says it is not wise to compare yourself by yourself. The question on the floor is "Why are you comparing?"

"For we dare not class ourselves or compare ourselves with some who commend themselves; but these, measuring themselves by themselves, and comparing themselves with themselves, are not intelligent." (II Corinthians 10:12)

"PKs, you living in *'Glass Houses'*. I encourage you to develop a personal, trusting relationship with the LORD of LORDS and KING of KINGS. Allow Him to heal you from the inside out. Come out of your shell. Retreating is not the answer. You are still on display. The best way to handle any situation is to face it.

Our Parents are not perfect and neither are we. In this life, we strive towards perfection. We have been forgiven by God, our Father. His Son, Jesus, died to redeem us and rose to justify us, more than 2000 years ago. Right now He is sitting at the Right Hand of God making intercession for us.

As quite as it is kept, *Preachers' Kids* are not the only people, *'Living in Glass Houses'*. Celebrities, Politicians, Athletes, Royalty and the like also *'live in glass houses';* however, their lives are under a microscope. We can close the door, pull down the shades and keep the Paparazzi out. We are not followed around with cameras, videos and audios. We can go to school, shopping, work and our places of worship without any problems. Many Celebrities, Royalty, Politicians and the like have people following them daily. That is not happening to us. Think about it. When you think your situation is bad, there is someone worst than you. Remember you are *"Living in a Glass House"*, but not under a microscope. Thank God, you can still breathe a sigh of relief.

There is greatness in you. Let God develop the gifts that is in you. There is Ministry in you. You have excellent communication skills, leadership skills, and musical skills, acts of kindness, and acting abilities.

As Children, the entire community raised us. If you were doing something wrong, an adult would correct you before you went home. When you arrived home, your Parents followed through on the discipline. So you can see, we have always lived in a *'Glass House'*. It was for our good, not detriment. Get over it. Some of them break the law and when they come looking for mercy and grace, it is not there.

Accept the fact that you are privileged to be born to parents who are members of The Reverend Clergy. It cannot be changed no matter how hard you wish it wasn't so. The same thing is true of your DNA. You can't change your biological Parents. Your life will be so much easier when you accept this fact. Ask God to order your steps. Accept God's guidance in every facet of your life. Trust God. He didn't make a mistake. He wasn't trying to be funny when He called your Parents into the service of Ministry.

In Biblical days, some of the members of the Tribe of Levi were the Priests. That tribe was set aside to meet the needs in the Synagogue. Some were Priests, some singers, some musicians, some were the makers of the priestly garments; some were builders; some cleaned the Synagogue, some were chefs. Some of them furnished the Synagogue. Whatever the need was in the Synagogue, a member of the Tribe of Levi was assigned to that Ministerial service or task. As a result, this was the only Tribe not given their own land grant when the Children of Israel entered the Promised

Land. Their portion of the Promised Land was in the Temple. They received a portion of the offerings brought into the Temple. All of their needs were met. They did not want for anything.

It was in the Mind of God for you to be a child of The Reverend Clergy. Be proud of your family. Your Parents could have been mass murderers, child abusers, derelicts, drug addicts, pimps, prostitutes, devil worshippers, members of cults, occults and the like. What would you have said about it? How would you feel if that was the case? Would that make you proud?

I know of a situation where a couple had several Children. Both of the Parents had good jobs. Every weekend they got drunk – so drunk in fact that they would fall into the streets. Their Children loved their Parents so much that they would go looking for their Parents and pick them up out of the streets and take them home. This scenario was played and replayed every weekend. Sometimes their Mom's private parts would be exposed. They would pull her skirt or dress down and take her home.

Today, most of those Children are in the Ministry and very prosperous in their choice of vocation. They did not have any illegitimate Children to my knowledge. Their Parents were alcoholics but somewhere they learned to respect their Parents and preserve through it all. I never heard a word of complaint from any of them. They held their heads high and became victors not victims.

This would have been too much for me to handle but they did. What about you? Could you take it? Would you have fallen apart? You have issues that your Parent(s) is a Minister. Pre-suppose, it was the other way around and they were hell raisers, what would you have done?

You might say, "Well, I will never know." I am sure you are glad about it. Take off your mask. First, "to thine own self be true". God has a plan for you and yours. He wants what is best for you. He will not do anything to harm you. There are many good and precious promises that have been given to us by God from Genesis to Revelations. Read and meditate on them. Apply them to your daily lives. Get rid of the attitude. Stop the victim mentality. Realize you were born from the best of the best. Psalm 139 tells us plainly that we were made in the image and likeness of God, our Father.

Pastors and Leaders, take inventory. Do not hold Church as usual. *"Seek ye first the kingdom of God and His righteousness (God's way of doing things) and all these things shall be added unto you."* (Matthew 6:33 AMP) Put God's Word first. Seek His Will with your whole heart. Develop a personal relationship with God. He loves you so much. He wants to teach you how to love Him and others. It is a matter of the heart, to love and receive love, in return.

Your Children are calling you hypocrites, liars and phonies because you talk love. When others are present, you demonstrate love to strangers in the street. Yet, you do not always demonstrate love in your own home, with your family. The question on the floor is: How do you justify that?

Love is what you do *not* what you say. My Godfather always said, *"What you do speak so loud I do not hear what you say."* Your speech betrays you. I encourage you to take inventory. Take off the mask. First, *"to your own self be true"*. You must be true to you, before; you can be true to me or anyone else. Bishops, Pastors, Priests, Rabbis, Elders, Missionaries, Deacons and all members of The Reverend Clergy; your Children and family members are crying out for your attention. They are desirous of spending quality time with you and/or their Parent(s).

Dad, you should spend some quality time with your daughter. Listen to her. Take her out on dates at least once a month. Show her how a man should treat a lady. Cater to her. You should open doors for your daughter when she is going into and out of buildings and cars. Always show her how valuable she is to you. Help her to realize her self worth. Encourage your daughter to always be a lady above reproach inside and outside of the home. Celebrate her, not tolerate her.

Dad, be an example, for your son and daughter. Show them how a man should love and care for his family (Wife and Children). Have family time with them at least once a week. Include your family in some of your devotion times. Have fun times with your family. You must never have more time for outsiders, than you have for your wife and Children. Always putting others first, can cause a lot of unnecessary grief, for you, your wife and Children.

Many times, Dad, you expect your family to understand why you are not spending quality time with them. But they do not. All they know is my Dad is more concerned about making sure others are cared for but gives little or no concern for us. Your Children are not just Children. They are your Children, your seed. They need you to show them that you care. It would not bother them that you are helping others, if your helping others, did not interfere with their lives.

If you do this, it will result in a lot less pain and suffering for your family, possibly the community and yourself. Give your Children some degree of normalcy as they live their lives. Your Ministerial duties are the same as a full-time job. Do not let it consume who you are. Remember: You are a man first with a family. You should attend their recitals, ball games and other extra curriculum activities. Take them to amusement parks, the zoo, the beach, the theatre and the like. Go on vacation with your family. Do not get too busy to play with them.

Example:

Michael, one of my nephews was watching a football game when his son, little Michael came into the room. He asked his Dad to come outside and play with him. His Dad responded in this manner. "I am watching the game." Little Mike's response to his Dad was "What is more important to you, Dad, the game or me?" His Dad didn't have to think twice about it. The words of his son cut deeply into his heart. The television went off and outside he went to spend quality time with his son.

111

Tell me. What would you have done? "Lo, *Children are an heritage of the LORD: and the fruit of the womb is his reward." Happy is the man that hath his quiver full of them:"* (Psalm 127:3, 5a) Remember, your Children did not ask to be born. You are responsible for their welfare. Give them the love they desire, need and deserve. The return on your investment of love will be immeasurable.

Bishop, Pastor, Rabbi, Priest, Evangelist, Missionary, Deacon and other Members of The Reverend Clergy: As the first family, you are role models to other families in the Houses of Worship and in the community. You are expected to be examples in so many things. You are the first to arrive to the Church and the last to leave. You should be a reflection of godliness to the world; teaching and showing others what to do. There are many lonely times, when Parents are not at home with their Children. In spite of that, the Cleric vocation and calling requires much attention and care to everyone; including family. There will be countless sweet times to cherish and enjoy at home, when the family is together. God sees us through all our challenges and dilemmas. Yet, Scripture says to cast our cares upon Him for He cares for us. God is good. God can enable us to enjoy precious moments with family, as well as those we are called to serve. As God's stewards, we must live by faith and trust Him to never leave us, nor forsake us.

You Are In Need Of A Healing

Chapter 17

The name Preachers' Kids, (PK) is used to refer to Children of The Reverend Clergy, also known as: Bishop, Pastor, Priest, Rabbi, Evangelist, Missionary, Deacon, and other Clerics. It is mainly used to describe the Offspring of The Reverend Clergy.

We, the Offspring of The Reverend Clergy, are held to a higher standard and often subjected to greater scrutiny than other children. People around them, including their Parents, often set higher moral and behavioral standards for these Children. Due to the greater visibility of these Children, their mistakes are often magnified and given extra attention. We are often treated differently from others. There are different sets of rules for The Preachers' Kids vs. other Children. Sometimes, this causes negative and disruptive behaviors to surface. We are often stereotyped as '*holier-than-thou. We think we are better than others*'. Preachers' Kids are accused of always Preaching to any and every one they encounter. We rebel when we are constantly picked upon by Church folk and people in the community. Sometimes, we may deny our Parents or just do wrong behind their backs.

How does the Offspring of The Reverend Clergy or Preachers' Kids withstand the pressure of the Congregation's expectations? And how does a member of The Reverend Clergy protect his or her family? You can't keep individuals from peering in, but you can stop them from destroying your Children's lives. Protect your Children from malicious nonsense. Protect them from the so called do-gooders. My Parents did everything imaginable to help their Children to live as unto the LORD, although we were *"Living in a Glass House"*. They did immeasurable things to help us grow as wholesome individuals. I thank God for both Mom and Dad. My siblings and I are blessed to have had them as our Parents. (O how I miss them. They have transitioned into their new home with the LORD).

We had family prayer at least once per week with my Dad leading the prayer. He would pray for our well being, our protection, our prosperity, as well as, our personal relationships with Jesus Christ, God's Son. We would all kneel and pray individually for a while. After which, Dad would lead us into corporate prayer. After which, Mom would lead us into a song. Dad and Mom prayed fervently for us during their individual prayer time. *"The effectual fervent prayer of a righteous man availeth much,"* (James 5:15b) They didn't know what was going on inside of us. But they had the presence of mind to have family meetings with us so we could discuss what was happening in our lives. In retrospect, I know it was the LORD ordering their steps. They put their trust in God to take care of us at all times. They knew we had need of the Holy Spirit to sustain us at all times.

During our family time, Dad would re-iterate that we should never let anyone put us down because of what we do or do not have, the color of our skin, our size or whatever. We are as good as or better than anyone walking on two feet. Those statements are as much a part of me today as they were when I was a child. He instilled in his Children the confidence that we needed to help us from day to day. Mom and Dad taught us to trust God with our whole hearts in all things. Take God at His Word.

Dad gave us the freedom to be Children. He let us play sports, go to the movies with our friends and family, laugh and have fun. We were given limited freedom. I overheard some ladies from the Church tell Dad, "Mom was going to make him go to hell, because we had those freedoms". But he was not moved by their remarks. He did not let them rule his home. Dad and Mom wanted us to be happy, well-rounded individuals. I thank God for giving us to them and them to us.

114

Man is born in sin and shapened in iniquity as everyone born into this world. As long as we live in these houses of clay, we are subject to sin. This flesh we are living in is an enemy of God. Dad stressed the importance of letting go and letting God have His way in our lives. He stressed the importance of transparency. We must tell him the truth. If he ever caught us in an untruth; it meant discipline for us. What did that mean? We would be chastised with love and self-control. When we failed at something, Dad and Mom were there to encourage us to try again. They did not hesitate to tell us how much they loved us and to show their love to each other in front of us. We did need to know that, in our failure, Dad and Mom loved and accepted us as we were; so does God our heavenly Father.

Dad always tried to protect us from the outside world. He was a very wise man. We knew he loved us and cared more deeply about us than the external appearance of his earthly ministry. Our parents never sent us on guilt trips. Dad was not bound by what people thought. He loved us and taught us Biblical principles.

Dad would assert his authority when Church members overstepped their boundaries where his family was concerned. He stood up in a Church meeting and made some statements about his family advising them to back off. Mom was his Spouse. We were his Children. My Dad quickly stepped in to protect his family. He didn't show favoritism toward his Kids in the Church, but he was willing to defend us when necessary. Before we would go to Church, Dad told us that we should not play with God. It didn't matter what the other Children did. We should not follow suit. If we did, Dad would give us a good licking when we went home. God is not a plaything. Do not play with God. Be real for God not a fake. We obeyed Dad because we knew he had our best interest at heart and it helped that we did not want a licking. Dad and Mom enforced the boundary between our family and our Church members. Their loving kindness and decisive action allowed us to follow our goals.

Reverend Clergy, allow your Children to explore what God has put in their hearts. My Parents were Spiritual Leaders. An entire Church, the community, and, the WJAY 1280 AM Radio listening audience, in South Carolina, looked to them for guidance. I was keenly aware of their status in the community, and to be honest, I didn't want to share them in the beginning with outsiders. Dad explained that the call of God on his life did not mean that he would not be there for us. I could go to my Dad for all things big or small.

Members of The Reverend Clergy have asked me, "How did you make it? How can I help my kids make it?" Ultimately, it's all about the Grace of God, but I'm also convinced that my Parents' application of the Word of God is why we are where we are today. I thank God for all He has done for us. Preachers' Kids, you are hurting. There are many negative feelings churning on the inside of you. I too, feel your pain. I had negative feelings because of the Church people making digs at me. One day I came to grips with the fact, that *'I am a King's Kid'*. There is nothing anyone can say that can change that fact. I do not have to feed into their issues. I know who I am. The scripture says, *"For we are God's [own] handiwork (His workmanship) recreated in Christ Jesus, [born anew] that we may do those good works which God predestined (planned beforehand) for us [taking paths which He prepared ahead of time], that we should walk in them [living the good life which He prearranged and made ready for us to live"*. (Ephesians 2:10 AMP)

Chapter 18

I want you to think of what it is like being a PK or Preachers' Kid? Did you at any time consider the other kids in the Church and or Synagogue who are not PKs? It seems to be okay for the Children of the Laity to behave a certain way. But if their Parents are members of The Reverend Clergy, they are looked upon as horrible people. How many times has a Preachers' Kid been told "You can't do this or that because people won't like it?" They won't understand.

How many Children of The Reverend Clergy missed out on a normal childhood, because their Parents would not let them experience life, because people might talk? You couldn't go to the movies; it just doesn't look right. If people see you at the movies or a sporting event, then they won't come to our Church. How many Preachers' daughters were made to wear dresses because "Preachers' daughters do not and/or should not dress like the world? How is wearing something other than a dress looking or dressing like the world?

Example:

My sisters and I had to wear dresses all of the time. When it was extremely cold, my Mom would put pants on us under our dresses. We had to take the pants off when we arrived at school. The Church women did not like it at all. My Parents were ridiculed because of it; they condemned my Dad to hell. During the summer, we would go to the beach. When we went to the beach, my sisters and I wore denim skirts and T-shirts. However, my brothers could wear shorts

117

but the girls, could not. Imagine the weight of denim in the 60's.
When the denim was wet, it was very heavy as we walked down the
beach. It felt like we were carrying a sack of potatoes. We were
wearing wet T-shirts on the beach before they were popular. Today,
I do not enjoy going to the beach, although I can wear what I
choose. We always had to set examples for every one in the
community including the Church.

Preachers' Kids weren't allowed to fall asleep in a Church
service. It didn't matter that all the other Children were asleep.
Question? Were not they also supposed to reverence God? If we
went to sleep in Church, we were awakened immediately. Other
Children could lie out on the benches and their Parents would not
wake them. It was okay. I call that a double standard.

Many PKs were not allowed to participate in sports at
school. Dad and Mom did allow us to play sports but many of the
Preachers Kids I have met later in life could not. Their parents were
doing God's work, and their after-school sport activity would
interfere with the Ministry. God might get angry if they didn't have
an evening service, but they went to a ball game. Some might say it
is sacrilegious. They are not raising their Children in the fear of
God. Preachers' Kids must always be in Church, but their Children
could stay home and go to ball games.

It wasn't always easy being a Preachers' Kid. Oftentimes we
are ignored because our Parent is ministering to other people. After
your parents had taken care of Ministerial responsibilities, they were
too tired to give their Children what they needed. As we grew into
adulthood, we become "miniature" Bishops, Pastors, Preachers,
Evangelists, Rabbis, Priests, Missionaries, Deacons, etc. We are
different. This lesson should be learned early in life. Many times
during Sunday School Class and Vacation Bible School when your
Mom (the Preachers wife) is teaching; the supplies are short, and
you, the Preachers' Kids may not get the necessary supplies. It was
imperative that the others were served first. It is okay if you do not
get one. You can tough it up and understand. Parents, realize, we
have feelings too. We are Children also. We want to feel special to

118

God, Jesus and the Holy Spirit. It is not fair to us. We are the ones that do not get the crafts and the trinkets in Vacation Bible School (VBS). We should understand that our Parents must reach others for Christ, but what about us. Parents, we have souls to be saved. Our feelings get hurt. We feel rejection. Do not save the world and your wife and Children are lost.

Our Parents are Ministers and for some reason the community expect us to be replicas of them. That means we skip our childhood. When the Worship Leader doesn't come to the service, we are to fill in. We are the Ushers. We are the Choir members. We are the Offering collectors or Trustees. We are the Deacons, until some come into the Church. At times, it is a lonely life as a Preachers' Kid. We are not invited to the parties, nor can we go to get-togethers outside of the Church.

The Parents hosting the get together don't want us to come to their homes, peradventure we tell the Minister Parent(s) what happens. The other Children are not permitted to tell us what happened at the party either. This is the scenario: the Children that attended the party are talking about it among themselves. You can hear them laughing and talking. You walk up and ask why they are laughing. Their reply is nothing. They look at each other and snicker. You feel worst than before you asked them. You feel ostracized.

Although these things are happening to us, we are expected to continue in the leadership roles at Church without fail. They tell us this: Remember people are watching you. The Children are often watched to ascertain how the family is living at home. Well-behaved, happy Kids signify a good Christian home. If you are misbehaving, and not actively involved in your Parents' Ministry, something is wrong with them (your Parents). They will throw a Scripture out that says *"If a man can't rule his household, how can he take care of the House of God?"* (See I Timothy 3:1-7) We are expected to be walking Bibles. We thought to be super spiritual and never rebellious. If we do anything that they feel we should not do, we are considered '*the worst kind*'.

119

What would make us rebel against our Parents? Do you think we awakened one day and decided I am going to rebel? Is it something we planned for a while? Were we forced into it? Is it a cry for help and/or attention from our Parents? What is it?

Consider this? It may be the only time we get attention from our Parents. When we are being reprimanded for something we were accused of, our Parents listened. Perhaps, at times, punishment filled the need to be recognized. As a result, we are seen as separate persons, apart from our Parents. We are tired of trying to be what others want us to be. We want to be different. We desire to be ourselves, not an image of our Parents.

Preachers' Kids sometimes get fed up, rebel and turn away from the Church as the prodigal son when he left home. But most of the time we do not go far. We realize there is nothing in the world but destruction. We go to these parties and the heathens at the party look at us and say, *"What are you doing here? You know you do not belong here."* Heathens know we do not belong, even when we are rebelling and trying to fit. After a while, we get sick and tired of being sick and tired and turn back to God and the things of God. He did not leave us. We left Him. It isn't long before we realize, no matter how far we go; God is still watching over us. If we get off track, experiment with things of the world; we have been grounded on Rock. We should repent and turn back to God, just as the prodigal son returned to his father.

Example:

A Preachers'Kid was sitting outside of the Church with her cousin, in a car, talking. She was later accused of smoking, by a Church member. This individual, hurriedly, told her Pastor Dad. She was chastised by her Parents. Soon after, it was discovered that the incident was not true. Some PKs may do drugs: legal and/or illegal; others get involved in premarital sex and/or whatever. Afterward, we are considered backsliders. It is a known Biblical saying, *"God is married to the backslider"*. We are expected to come to ourselves. We are then encouraged to repent and return to God.

Remorse and repentance is all that is required. God is perceived as a loving Father, waiting for His Children with open arms.

Don't be so hard on a Preachers' Kid, just because Dad is a member of The Reverend Clergy. Just because the family is in Ministry doesn't make them any less of a Kid. So, don't be so hard on PKs. Remember, oftentimes, Preachers' Kids have never had a childhood. The Cleric has been too busy dealing with needs of Parishioners, to spend as much time, with his family, as he would have liked. Why don't you make a special effort to pray for the Preacher, the Spouse and the Kids? Perhaps, you can pitch in, by offering to spend time with them. After all, their Parents do so much for you and the community.

How do I know these feelings and such? That's easy; I'm a Preacher's Kid. If you are one also, you might want to celebrate the life you were given. Let's stop bellyaching and embrace the family business. It is not always the pulpit. It is a worldwide, day after day Ministry. The family business is in need of, behind the scenes, specialty people such as tech and support. Everyone is not called to the front line. We need all you, from across America and around the world to strengthen the PK alliance. Let's continue to grow from "strength to strength". (See Psalm 84:7)

The Great Commission: *"And He [Jesus] said unto them, Go ye into all the world, and preach the gospel to every creature"*.

(Mark 16:15)

We must allow God to rise up in us, through us and by us. Preachers' Kids, I know you are hurting. At times, there are countless negative feelings, churning on the inside of us. I, also, feel the pain of caring for others. Pain hurts no matter who is suffering. "Rise Up O'God, hear the voice of Preachers' Kids, show Yourself strong on our behalf." Thank You LORD for calling our Parents and families. We are grateful to You for choosing us as PKs.

Scriptures to Encourage You

"And the afflicted people Thou wilt save: but Thine eyes are upon the haughty, that Thou mayest bring them down."
(II Samuel 22:28)

"Thou shalt hide them in the secret of Thy presence from the pride of man: Thou shalt keep them secretly in a pavilion from the strife of tongues." (Psalm 31:20)

"For the sin of their mouth and the words of their lips let them even be taken in their pride: and for cursing and lying which they speak."
(Psalm 59:12)

"Surely men of low degree are vanity, and men of high degree are a lie: to be laid in the balance, they are altogether lighter than vanity." (Psalm 62:9)

"Whoso privily slandereth his neighbour, him will I cut off: him that hath an high look and a proud heart will not I suffer."
(Psalm 101:5)

"Lord, my heart is not haughty, nor mine eyes lofty: neither do I exercise myself in great matters, or in things too high for me."
(Psalm 131:1)

"Though the LORD be high, yet hath He respect unto the lowly: but the proud He knoweth afar off." (Psalm 138:6)

"The fear of the LORD is to hate evil: pride, and arrogancy, and the evil way, and the froward mouth, do I hate."
(Proverbs 8:13)

"When pride cometh, then cometh shame: but with the lowly is wisdom." (Proverbs 11:2)

Scriptures to Encourage You
(continued)

"Pride goeth before destruction, and an haughty spirit before a fall." (Proverbs 16:18)

"Better it is to be of an humble spirit with the lowly, than to divide the spoil with the proud." (Proverbs 16:19)

"Before destruction the heart of man is haughty, and before honor is humility." (Proverbs 18:12)

"Most men will proclaim every one his own goodness: but a faithful man who can find?" (Proverbs 20:6)

"Proud and haughty scorner is his name, who dealeth in proud wrath." (Proverbs 21:24)

"There is a generation that are pure in their own eyes, and yet is not washed from their filthiness." (Proverbs 30:12)

"Better is the end of a thing than the beginning thereof: and the patient in spirit is better than the proud in spirit."
(Ecclesiastes 7:8)

"Extol not thyself in the counsel of thine own heart; that thy soul be not torn in pieces as a bull [straying alone.]"
(Ecclesiastes 6:2)

"The Lord only is righteous, and there is none other but He,"
(Ecclesiastics 18:2)

"He that findeth his life shall lose it: and he that loseth his life for My sake shall find it." (Matthew 10:39)

Scriptures to Encourage You
(continued)

"But we are all as an unclean thing, and all our righteousnesses are as filthy rags; and we all do fade as a leaf; and our iniquities, like the wind, have taken us away." (Isaiah 64:6)

"But go ye and learn what that meaneth, I WILL HAVE MERCY, AND NOT SACRIFICE: for I am not come to call the righteous, but sinners to repentance." (Matthew 9:13)

Prayer

Father in Jesus Name,

I confess it is not always easy to obey our Parents. Sometimes, I think they are wrong. I can only obey them with Your help. Help me. I desire to obey Your Word and be in compliance with Your Will. I am looking unto You, Jesus, the Author and Finisher of my faith. Give me all that I have need of, to be who You want me to be.

Father, I ask this in Jesus Name. Amen.

I trust in You, LORD with my whole heart. I will not lean unto my own understanding. Help me to be a blessing on a daily basis. I desire Your perfect will to be done in my life. I love you LORD. Use me for Your glory. In Jesus Name. Amen. Amen.

Chapter 19

Let me encourage you with these words.

God loves you. He has chosen you for a time and a purpose to bring honor to Him. God has His hands on our lives. We were covered by God before we were born. You and your family have been objects of satanic attack. He is trying to destroy you by using people in your inner circle: family, friends, classmates, neighbors, colleagues, teachers, Church members, as well as those in authority.

These people have allowed the enemy to use their mouths to anesthetize you. Their words were poisonous as they spewed out of their mouths. James tells us, *"The tongue is full of deadly poison. Therewith we bless God and curse man. This shouldn't be. Out of the same mouth proceed blessings and cursings."* (See James 3:2-10) Some of these people profess to love you but their words say something different.

You now have low self-esteem. You feel inadequate, unsure of yourself, less than a man, less than a woman. You have forgotten that you are made in the image and likeness of God our Father. In the Book of the beginnings, Genesis, we find this truth. God molded man into His image blew the breath of life into him and man became a living soul. Didn't you know that God did not make a mistake when He formed you? God knows your end from your beginning. He is acquainted with all your ways.

God the Father, God the Son, God the Holy Spirit, three in one, is always looking out for you. He wants me to remind you of your importance to Him. You are the 'Apple of His eye'. He is not trying to take any thing away from you. He wants to give you all you need and so much more.

Those Anesthetizes told you that you were a mistake, a nothing, will never be nothing, but the devil is a liar and the father of lies. God is the giver and sustainer of life. You are not a surprise to Him. If the truth be told, you are not a surprise to your Parents. They knew what it would take to make a baby before you were conceived. Do not get caught up in negative rhetoric about your conception. You are here by the Grace of God. He is keeping you on a daily basis from dangers seen and unseen, even in your foolishness.

God is keeping you in the good and bad times. You may have walked away from God and the things of God, but He is still looking out for you. He is opening doors that have been closed in your face. Didn't you know that you are the righteousness of God in Christ Jesus? Children of The Reverend Clergy, come home today. Reclaim your inheritance. Take back what the devil stole from you.

While I was visiting South Carolina a few years ago, I saw a former classmate of one of my sisters. He said to me, *You were voted least likely to succeed.* He was not in my class. He tried to date me when we were younger. Now this drunkard is standing before me with nonsense. My response was: "*Maybe that was your vote, but God. You may have counted me out, but God. I am so glad you are not in control of my destiny.*" His reply, "*I can see that I was wrong*". I began to share with him the Good News about Jesus. Of course, he did not want to hear it, so he left hurriedly.

Words from Another Anesthesizer

Arnetha, girl, it is so good to see you. You all are doing a good job, helping your Mother. Mother Bowens wears very nice clothes. Every one can see how well you all take care of her. I stood there smiling, and letting her know that Mother Bowens is my friend. She took care of us along with Dad, so it is our time to take care of her. Here is the clincher: *"You show look good, but you are so fat"* My response was: *"We can't all be small like Mom. Some of us had to take after my Dad"*. What happened? She repeated what she had said, initially, about my size. The third time she said it, was too much for me to handle.

I was trying to be nice and remind her of this truth that my Dad, Bishop Bowens, was a large man. But it was not working, so I decided to nip this in the bud. I thought about the scripture that says, *"Agree with thine adversary quickly whilst you are in the way with him"*. My next words were: *I might be fat, but . The But negated every thing I said first. I cancelled satan's plots and* plans for me. I pulled down his strongholds. My entire sentence was: *I might be fat, but I am so fine.* Her response: *"Girl you are something else"*. I said, *"Yes, maam. I am my Mom and Dad's daughter"*. Her response, *"I better let you go Mother Bowens is probably waiting for you"*. I hugged her and off I went. This happened years ago. From that time to this, she has never mentioned another word to me about my size. I see her sometimes when I go home, but my size does not come up any more.

While living in Pennsylvania, a supposed friend came to visit. After we embraced she said, "You are always changing your hair. One day it is short; one day it is long. I do not know what to expect from you from day to day. Do you push a button on your back like they do on doll babies to make their hair long or short"? It was time to nip this foolishness in the bud. I laughed and said: *"Variety is the spice of life. I am so glad with the hair that is on my head. I can do with it as I please. I have choices"*. It was none of her business what I did with the hair on my head. As I write this chapter, I am reminded of a statement my Aunt Dollie Mae used to say, *"Give me back my business"*. Aren't you tired of folk minding your business? You can't stop them from talking but you can get them out of your business.

When I turned fifty plus, someone called to wish me a Happy Birthday. Their question, *"Did you ever think you would turn fifty plus? What do you mean? Yes. I thought I would turn this age. As a matter of fact, I expect to live until I am (120) one hundred twenty. Longevity runs in my family"*. She shut her mouth. I am tired of the devil. How about you? If you are not paying close attention, he will have you agreeing with nonsense, putting natural laws into motion. These laws are put into motion by the seeds that you sow out of your mouths. *"Death and life are in the power of your own tongue:"* (See Proverbs 18:21a) Remember, your own tongue. It is not what I say about you, it is what you say about you.

Children of the Reverend Clergy (CoTRC), First, "to thine own self be true". It is time to take off the mask. Be real with yourself. Take responsibility for your own position in this life. Forgive the offenders. Return to God. Let Him heal your wounds. He is a healer of the broken heart. Let Him heal you from the inside out. Cast all of your cares upon the Lord. Cry out to God. Tell Him all about your hurts, pains, disappointments and rejections. Take it all to the Cross where Jesus hung, bled and died for you. Ask God to forgive you and help your unforgiveness.

Chapter 20

No more excuses. No more excuses. No more excuses. It is time to come out of Lodebar where you have been hiding. Come and take your rightful place at the King's table. You have been in Lodebar far too long. The feast has been prepared. The table has been set. God has prepared a table before you in the presence of your enemies. It is time to come and dine. Read Genesis 9. It tells a story of David looking for someone in Saul's family that he could show kindness.

Mephibosheth, Jonathan's son, was hiding in Lodebar. His nurse hid him because she was afraid that he would be killed. David sent for him and restored him to Royalty. CoTRC, Lodebar is not the place for you. You were chosen by God to be strong and do exploits. All the plots and plans of the devil have been done away. God sent His only Begotten Son – Jesus to pay the debt in full. When Jesus said, *It is finished,* while hanging on the Cross, it was indeed finished. The price to redeem mankind back to God has been paid in full. All of your needs have been met. The curse has been reversed. Your enemy has been defeated. Every stronghold has been broken off of your life. Every generational curse cancelled. The sacrifice has been received as a sweet smell in the nostrils of Almighty God. Jesus broke the curse off of our lives. The curse of poverty, lack, sickness, disease and infirmities has been broken – once and for all. When Jesus said, *It is finished.* That means, everything He came into the earth to accomplish was complete.

129

When people try to speak negative words over your life, do not receive them. You are as good as or better than anyone walking on two feet – my Dad – Bishop Bowens always said. Never let anyone put you down because of anything.

Pastor Andrae Crouch, penned a song, years ago that says: *"Through it all. I have learned to trust in Jesus. I have learned to trust in God. Through it all, I have learned to depend upon His Word."* Trust God today with your whole heart. You can always depend upon His Word.

No problem can break you unless you let it. You have to sign for it. Meaning – If you do not make the issues yours, they will not affect you. May the blessing of the Lord that make rich and add no sorrow continue to be with you and yours today, tomorrow, this week, this month, this year and the rest of your lives. Take God at His word. He watches over His Word to perform it.

"Yes indeed, it won't be long now. God's Decree. Things are going to happen so fast your head will swim one thing fast on the heels of the other. You won't be able to keep up. Everything will be happening at once—and everywhere you look blessings! Blessings like wine pouring off the mountains and hills. I'll make everything right again for my people."

"They'll rebuild their ruined cities. They'll plant vineyards and drink good wine. They'll work their gardens and eat fresh vegetables. And I'll plant them, plant them on their own land. They'll never again be uprooted from the land I've given them."

(Amos 9:13-15 MSG)

LORD, Your Word, says so.

Look for it! It is yours! It is ours! Hallelujah!!!

It is my sincere prayer that this book has made, will make and is making a positive difference in your life. I love you with the love of the LORD. "Go Forth and Prosper." Enjoy, Arnetha.

Words of Encouragement:

Bishop Joseph P. Bowens

Chapter 21

Change your thinking; change your life. Change your life; change your destiny. Your thoughts a ffect your a ttitude; your mood, as well as your future. Thoughts can make you miserable; in turn, you make others miserable. Thoughts can make you happy; in turn, you make others happy. Philippians 4:8 tell us plainly what we should think on. *"Finally, brethren, whatsoever things are true, whatsoever things are honest, whatsoever things are just, whatsoever t hings are pure, whatsoever things are lovely, whatsoever things are of good report; if there be any virtue, and if there be any praise, think on these things."* Stop vacillating between two opinions. There is a battle going on for and in the minds of men, women, boys and girls.

Satan is a deceiver and a liar. He wants you to blame external forces for all of your misery when in actuality; you are the culprit. Introspection is needed on a regular basis. Think about what you are allowing to take up residency in your mind. Erase all negative mind chatter. No matter the struggle, anticipate payday which is the day when this will all be over. When sufferings are compared with payday there is no comparison. Your light afflictions are not to be compared to the Glory that shall be revealed in us. This too shall pass sooner rather than later.

God is preparing you for your destiny. What you are going through at this time is called life. Life happens to every one of us.

Renew your mind with the Word of God in accordance with Romans 12:1-2. Explore ways to take yourself away from your situation and your troubles. Dare to dream. There is something better. Learn from the challenges of yesterday. What you are going through is temporary. Today is another day.

Ask the LORD to renew your mind. Let me say this again. Be not conformed to this world, but be transformed by the renewing of your mind. There is something better. You do not have to settle. Do not allow anyone to dictate to you. Believe in God and yourself. God has the last say. It doesn't matter what people say; but God. You will realize suddenly that you can lead as well as follow. Through all of your trials, test, temptation and tribulation, know God has it all under His control.

Know this: You can be in Church and out of Church at the same time. It is a mind thing. But thank God for salvation. Don't give up. Keep praying. Before long, you will see God turn it around for you. Aren't you glad the LORD gave you a chance? Aren't you glad the LORD saved you? Before it is too late, will you turn your life over to Jesus? God specializes in things that seem to be impossible.

You have been hanging out in the chicken coup with chickens. Every time you try to fly, there is some negativity. Someone is telling you that it will not and/or cannot work. Stop hanging out with chickens. You are an eagle. Throw those chickens some chicken feed. You go on and soar on wings of an eagle to heights unknown.

Rise Up Father God. Hear the Voice of Your Children. Show Yourself Strong in Every Facet of Our Lives. Amen.

"Rise up, LORD, and let Thine enemies be scattered; and let them that hate Thee flee before Thee." (Numbers 10:35b)

132

A Useful Study Reference

Bible Verses Cited

Acknowledgments
Matthew 19:14

Welcome
Proverbs 10:22
Psalm 34:8

Chapter One
Luke 22:54b-60a
Proverbs 22:1
Psalm 25:2
Psalm 19:14

Chapter Two
John 10:10

Chapter Three
Proverbs 6:31
II Corinthians 10:12

Chapter Four
Psalm 99:12

Chapter Five
Luke 11:1b, 4
Matthew 5:12
Matthew 6:14-15
Jeremiah 29:11
Job 3:25
John 8:32, 36
I Peter 5:7
Matthew 18:18-20 MSG; 18:19

Bible Verses Cited

Chapter Six
Psalm 118:24
Psalm 37:23
Hebrews 13:5-6 MSG
Isaiah 40:31
John 8:36
1 Samuel 30:8
Micah 6:8

Chapter Seven
Nehemiah 6:1-4
Ephesians 6:12
II Corinthians 2:11
John 10:10
Nehemiah 8:10d
Psalm 101:7
Proverbs 6:16-19
I Peter 5:8
Luke 4:4-10
Ephesians 6:12
Matthew 6:33
James 4:7
Hebrews 1:2-3
Mark 14:38
Proverbs 10:22

Chapter Eight
John 10:10
Matthew 12:37
Romans 12:1-2
Philippians 2:5
Galatians 5:16

Chapter Eight (Cont.)
James 4:6
I Peter 5:5
I John 2:15-17
Proverbs 8:13
Ephesians 2:10 NASB
Isaiah 43:18-21
II Corinthians 5:17
Psalm 51:10-15
Luke 18:13
Jeremiah 30:17a
Exodus 15:26e; 23:25

Chapter Nine
I Corinthians 3:9
Job 22:28
Matthew 12:37
Proverbs 18:21 AMP
Psalm 101
Philippians 3:13-14
Proverbs 3:5-6 AMP
II Corinthians 10: 5
Jude 20
Galatians 6:7
Romans 10:3; 12:3
I Corinthians 3:21; 4:7
II Corinthians 10:5
Philippians 2:3; 3:19
I Timothy 3:6
II Timothy 3:2
James 1:17; 2:9

Chapter Ten
Job 22:28

Chapter Ten (Cont.)
Philippians 4:19
Revelations 3:20
Luke 15:11-32
Joel 2:25

Chapter Eleven
James 1:5
Mark 16:15-16
Hebrews 4:15
Acts 16:31
II Corinthians 6:2
Psalm 42:1
Romans 8:35
Psalm 34:8
Joel 2:25-26
Proverbs 11:30
II Corinthians 3:16-17
Hebrews 12:2
Proverbs 4:22, 26 AMP
Ephesians 6:12 AMP
II Timothy 1:7 AMP
Galatians 3:13 AMP
Hebrews 4:12 AMP; 4:14
James 4:7 AMP
Romans 8:28
I Peter 5:7
Proverbs 23:7
Philippians 3:13-14
II Corinthians 10:5
Matthews 6:14-15
Isaiah 43:25-26
Romans 12:2
Isaiah 43:18-19

134

Chapter Eleven (Cont.)
Psalm 43:5
Philippians 4:8
Hebrews 13:6
James 4:7-8a
Genesis 1:1

Chapter Twelve
Jeremiah 9:23-24
Psalm 23:1
Isaiah 26:3-4
Romans 12:13
Jeremiah 1:5, 8
Matthew 25:40
Leviticus 20:7
James 1:19 AMP
Proverbs 18:13
I Thessalonians 4:11-12
Proverbs 10:19 AMP
John 5:2-9
Matthew 9:37-38
I Timothy 6:6-8
Exodus 20:12
Galatians 5:22-23 AMP
Hebrews 10:23

Chapter Thirteen
Revelation 3:8
John 15:16
Philippians 1:6
Proverbs 10:22
Isaiah 43:18-19
Psalm 23:5
I Corinthians 2:9

Chapter Thirteen (Cont.)
Isaiah 55:11
Psalm 91:10-11; 34:7
I Peter 2:24 AMP
Matthew 8:17 AMP
Isaiah 53:4-5 AMP
Romans 8:2 AMP
II Corinthians 10:4 AMP
Ephesians 6:11, 16 AMP
Psalm 91:1 AMP
Psalm 112:7 AMP
Exodus 15:26 AMP
Deuteronomy 32:39
Psalm 90:1-2

Chapter Fourteen
Matthew 6:33
II Timothy 2:15
Galatians 5:7
Psalm 46:10; 115:14-15
II Corinthians 2:11
John 10:10
Proverbs 18:22
Genesis 2:24
Joel 2:25
Psalm 23:4; 27:1
II Timothy 1:7
II Corinthians 10:5
Luke 9:11
Matthew 6:33

Chapter Fifteen
I Peter 5:7
Philippians 4:8

Bibel Verses Cited

Bible Verses Cited

Chapter Fifteen (Cont.)
Isaiah 49:15b-16 AMP
II Timothy 1:7
Psalm 23:4
Hebrews 13:5-6
Psalm 27:1
II Timothy 1:7
I John 4:18
II Corinthians 10:5
Luke 9:11
Matthew 6:33
Psalm 27
Habakkuk 2:2-4
II Thessalonians 5:18
Ephesians 1:18

Chapter Sixteen
I Kings 19:11-12
Isaiah 30:5a
Ephesians 6:12
II Corinthians 10:12
Matthew 6:33 AMP
Psalm 127:3, 5a

Chapter Seventeen
James 5:15b
Ephesians 2:10 AMP

Chapter Eighteen
I Timothy 3:1-7
Psalm 84:7
Mark 16:15
II Samuel 22:28
Psalm 31:20; 59:12
Psalm 62:9; 101:5

Chapter Eighteen (Cont.)
Psalm 131:1; 138:6
Proverbs 8:13; 11:2
Proverbs 16:18-19
Proverbs 18:12; 20:6
Proverbs 21:24; 30:12
Ecclesiastes 7:8
Ecclesiastes 6:2; 18:2
Matthew 10:39
Isaiah 64:6
Matthew 9:13

Chapter Nineteen
James 3:2-10
Proverbs 18:21a

Chapter Twenty
Genesis 9
Amos 9:13-15 MSG

Chapter Twenty One
Philippians 4:8
Romans 12:1-2
Numbers 10:35b

About the Author
Romans 1:16-17

**An Offering Unto
The LORD**
Psalm 118:23-24
Proverbs 3:9-10
Psalm 68:11
Benediction
II John 3, 4

ABOUT THE AUTHOR

ARNETHA BOWENS is the eighth child, of Bishop George Law Bowens Jr. and Mother Mary Ruth Bowens (God bless their memory.) She is a daughter of The Palmetto State of South Carolina; a true 'Southern Belle'. Arnetha is continuing her Parents' Ministry Legacy: *"Feeding the Hungry Souls: Outreach Ministry for Christ"* Program on WJAY Radio 1280 AM, in South Carolina. She is on Radio every Sunday afternoon at four o'clock. She can also be heard every second Sunday morning at 9:30 a.m. on the Smith/Cooper Program. It is indeed an honor and privilege having been bequeathed this sacred opportunity. The joy of walking and working in my Parent's founding tradition is a treasured blessing.

Desiring to make a difference in the lives of fellow PKs prompted her to write this book. Arnetha loves people. She has a compassionate concern for mankind. It is her desire to motivate, encourage and bring joy, whenever and wherever possible. She has been in communiqué with and has taken the love of God to many hurting people. Arnetha loves the Lord with all her heart. She is not ashamed to tell men, women, boys and girls about the Lordship of Jesus Christ. When you are having challenges, she will pray for and with you anytime and at anyplace.

Rev. Dr. Bowens is a consecrated Evangelist, a Pulpit Preacher and Motivational Speaker. Listen to her weekly Radio broadcasts. Follow her on Facebook and the Internet. Attend her classroom seminars, workshops and discussion groups.

"For I am not ashamed of the Gospel of Christ: for it is the power of God unto salvation to every one that believeth; to the Jew first, and also to the Greek. For therein is the righteousness of God revealed from faith to faith: as it is written, THE JUST SHALL LIVE BY FAITH." (Romans 1:16-17)

An Offering Unto the Lord

"This is the LORD's doing; it is marvelous in our eyes. This is the day which the LORD hath made; we will rejoice and be glad in it." (Psalm 118:23-24)

LORD, I Honor You with the Firstfruits of this Book. Use this Offering for Your Glory. Bless Your People and all Humanity in accordant to Proverbs 3:9-10.

"Honor the LORD with thy substance, and with the firstfruits of all thine increase: So shall thy barns be filled with plenty, and thy presses shall burst out with new wine."

Being called by God to Ministry, I am not ashamed to tell men, women, boys and girls about the Lordship of Jesus Christ. Where people are hurting and/or facing trials and challenges, I am willing to pray for them, anyplace and at anytime. Amen.

"The LORD gave the Word: great was the company of those that published it." (Psalm 68:11)

❧❧ ❦❦

BENEDICTION

"Grace be with you, mercy, and peace, from God the Father, and from the LORD Jesus Christ, the Son of the Father, in truth and love. I rejoiced greatly that I found of thy Children walking in truth, as we have received a commandment from the Father." (II John 3, 4)